SEACOAST MAINE

PEOPLE AND PLACES

Martin Dibner

Photographs by George A. Tice

SEACOAST MAINE

PEOPLE AND PLACES

Doubleday & Company, Inc., Garden City, New York

BOOKS BY MARTIN DIBNER

Fiction

THE BACHELOR SEALS

THE DEEP SIX

SHOWCASE

SLEEPING GIANT

A GOD FOR TOMORROW

THE ADMIRAL

THE TROUBLE WITH HEROES

Non-fiction

THE ARTS IN CALIFORNIA

SEACOAST MAINE *(with George A. Tice)*

PORTLAND *(Editor and designer)*

BOOKS BY GEORGE A. TICE

FIELDS OF PEACE *(with Millen Brand)*

GOODBYE RIVER GOODBYE *(with George Mendoza)*

PATERSON

SEACOAST MAINE *(with Martin Dibner)*

Excerpt from "Island People" from the book *Narration* by Gertrude Stein. Copyright 1935 by University of Chicago. Reprinted by permission of the University of Chicago Press.

Portion of "Winter Headland" by Louis O. Coxe from *The Wilderness and Other Poems*, by Louis O. Coxe. Copyright © 1958 by University of Minnesota. Reprinted by permission of University of Minnesota Press, Minneapolis.

Quotation from *Death in the Afternoon* by Ernest Hemingway. Reprinted by permission of Charles Scribner's Sons.

DESIGN AND SEQUENCE OF *SEACOAST MAINE* BY EARL TIDWELL

ISBN: 0-385-08849-3

Library of Congress Catalog Card Number 72-89412

"... the good and the bad, the ecstasy,
the remorse and sorrow, the people and places,
and how the weather was."

— HEMINGWAY

To my son Christopher

                         – G.T.

CONTENTS

INTRODUCTION

Maine is a country divided in three parts—the Maine coast, Aroostook County, the rest of Maine. By lumping this last into one category I do not mean to downgrade a pleasing countryside of winding back roads, lakes and rolling hills. Or its noble mountains and forests. Or the small farms and villages stubbornly rooted for a hundred years or more between the mill towns and burgeoning cities.

This rest of Maine, where I've lived for almost thirty years, is a hallowed terrain ranging from Sarah Orne Jewett's South Berwick through Hawthorne's Sebago Lake region and Harriet Beecher Stowe's Brunswick to Thoreau's enduring Ktaadn. But its character does not carry the sinewy identity or rugged impact of the other two. Aroostook's sprawling landscape, with fifty-mile sunsets and a man's winter shadow at noon twenty feet long, forewarns the new arrival he has come upon a stranger land. It is still a vast, unfashioned frontier with closer ties at times to Canada than to America and unlike any other region of New England. In physical shape and spirit and in the temper of its people it strongly resembles the turn-of-century Far West.

The Maine coast, to whose people and places most of these pages are devoted, is something else. An uncut original, you might say, in the old-fashioned meaning that implies the eccentric as much as it does a source and a beginning.

The coast itself may be divided into the area south of Portland, Portland itself and Down East. I had no idea, when I undertook this work, of the limitless range and depth of its substance. One could write on Maine forever, so fruitful a land of lore it is and its fascination so infinite.

JOURNAL NOTE: I have just taken a good look at the state's official highway map and report for the record that Maine resembles a huge, snaggled tooth pitted with a thousand cavities (its lakes), and with many jagged roots dangling in the cold sea. The

coastline from Kittery to Eastport (235 miles as the crow flies) inch by inch is 3,500 miles long.

Let it be clear from the start, this is no guidebook for tourists, no campground directory-cum-clam chowder recipes. A visitor to Maine seeking out-of-the-way antiques will find no clues in these pages. It's outrage enough a noun so venerable should be vulgarized into a predatory present participle and I'll give neither aid nor comfort to these pillagers.

One will find, I expect, as much enjoyment in George Tice's photographs as I did. Though it's his first confrontation with the scene, George has captured the Maine mystique on film with astonishing insight. Observe Dwight Stanley, Dean Emeritus of Monhegan lobstermen, truculent in mid-conversation behind his cribbage board. The stark beauty of winter tree forms near Deer Isle. A sea cliff on Mount Desert reminding one of the Wailing Wall in Jerusalem. The Shaker sisters at their noontime meal. Lew Dietz reminiscing. Any of these might inspire an essay, even a novel. And perhaps one will.

It may seem presumptuous of me, an inlander (and worse, not native-born), to write about the Maine coast. How can an outsider possibly know what it's *really* like? I don't. Nobody does, *really*. No two places are alike. But I know people. I like people. And people soon find that out and relax and talk easily about themselves. They trust me and, loving them and Maine, I trust my words to speak the truth. And if that isn't enough to silence purist grumblings, George Tice's pictures will surely do the job.

No geographic order follows. I came and went by wandering and whim, looking and listening, jotting down journal notes. Sometimes with George and sometimes alone. Certain voices sang clearly for me. Certain places cried out for the telling. Even whisperings, like the hum of insects in the Cathedral Woods and ghostly voices in abandoned boatyards are here distinct and unblurred. Maine is like that.

I spoke with lobstermen, painters, housewives, storekeepers, poets, island dwellers. People who create and people who destroy. A year's portfolio of humanity at times intriguing, tragic, funny, confusing, tied together with love and nostalgia. Like the workbench in a country barn, cluttered with tools and disemboweled farm gear, or a field of crusty lobster pots stacked like cordwood and surrounded by a collection of scarred buoys, grapnel and coiled fishing gear stiff with sea salt—all so wildly unreasonable as to seem exotic.

Yet all are indigenous to the Maine way. A gentle confusion that rightly belongs where it is. Maine people move slower than most and take more time to figure things out. They make fewer mistakes. They can scarcely afford either the risk or luxury of one. They share one thing in common. They choose to be where they are. They would rather be here than anywhere else in the world.

Finally, this is an affectionate appreciation of people and places I admire and love for their plain and decent ways, their downright horse sense and their damned integrity. But it's only a sampling. I wish I could have reached more of them and listened to their slow talk and put down their thoughts and feelings. There is no end to the surprise and delight it would provide.

A curious quality I found in the gruff Maine character is a surprising tenderness where it's least expected. Men use words like *love* and *dear* with a casual frequency that would have worried their Puritan forebears. When I first heard the affectionate terms, it gave me a few uneasy moments. A carpenter on a construction job sang out to his helper, "Pass me up the power saw, dear, would you now?" And when he got it: "Now that's a love."

It couldn't be more innocent or harmless. It's a mood of sheer joy one gets in Maine with the sun warming one's bones and green shoots pushing their sprouts through the moist spring earth. We do not speak enough with words like *love* and *dear*. We've bypassed tenderness in the dehumanizing transition from nature to push-button, self-service living. We've lost something precious along the way.

But not in Maine we haven't.

ISLAND PEOPLE

Every day their daily island living every day.
–GERTRUDE STEIN

Visitors to Maine are often surprised to discover islands off the coast with people actually living year round on them. Maine people of course know all about their offshore islands but surprisingly little about the life style of the inhabitants. One thing they find out sooner or later: Island people are "some different."

In her affectionate book *Maine Ways,* Elizabeth Coatsworth tells us island people develop very definite characteristics, ". . . sometimes bad but usually good." She finds them ". . . old fashioned, franker than mainland people, more individualistic and racier."

So they are. But I'd find it risky to be racy in the tight entanglement of an island grapevine. Other traits typical of island dwellers are their maddening contentment and a fierce sense of independence. "How can you live like this," the visitor asks, "without electricity, with rationed water . . . ?" The islander shrugs. All he asks of the summer tourists is that they leave the island as unspoiled as they found it.

Some of Maine's islands (there are 2,500 or so) are close enough to the mainland to be reached by causeway or bridge—islands like Mount Desert and Deer Isle, for example. The Casco Bay islands, Peaks, Long and Chebeague, in the vicinity of Portland are practically suburbia. Ferries run to them on regular daily schedules and also serve as sightseeing vessels. The larger offshore islands farther east, like Islesboro, Vinalhaven, North Haven, and Isle au Haut; Swan's Island, off Mount Desert; and tiny Matinicus and Monhegan, are also served by ferries, the schedule depending on the season and sometimes the weather.

Of all the Maine islands I favor Monhegan, a solitary whale couchant in a blue field of sea, sixteen miles distant with nothing beyond but more sea and the coast of France.

It was the Irish monk Brendan (or Brenainn) who first sailed into Monhegan's harbor in A.D. 565, following a visit to the hitherto unknown Canary Islands, then called the Fortunate Isles. His renown as a bold explorer established, he became the hero of a folk legend and a saint. Pre-Columbus charts show a "Saint Brendan's country" as the area of his alleged geographical discoveries. His feast day is May 16.

Brendan was followed by Norsemen, then by Basque, Portuguese and Breton fishermen, adventurers and sea traders, to whom the island's awesome cliffs became a landmark and its harbor a refuge.

On May 17, 1605, a Friday, James Rosier, a gentleman historian in the sailing ship *Archangel*, Captain George Waymouth commanding, described his first impression of Monhegan as ". . . a meane, high land, as after we found it, being but an Iland of some six miles in compasse, but I hope the most fortunate ever yet discovered."

And to wind up its history, about which this book is not, Charles Francis Jenney, three hundred and seventeen years after Rosier, concludes an historical monograph entitled *The Fortunate Island of Monhegan* with, "Where in years gone by sheep clambered, easels of artists now stand. From far and wide, seekers for rest and inspiration come, and never in vain. Its beautiful woodlands, waving moors, picturesque buildings, grand headlands, restless, mighty, and eternal sea, interpreted by the genius of the artist, delight thousands the country over. In verity it has been a fortunate island."

That being fifty-one years ago, in verity, it's still a fortunate island. But how long can it hold out against the inevitable desecration of man? The fir, beech, oak and birch are still there, forbidden by law to be cut. The moors and the grand headlands are weathering well. Some of the buildings remain picturesque at considerable cost to their owners who love them. Other dwellings, more recently built, sometimes mar the architectural unity of the place. There are fewer easels, easel painting having slipped somewhat from vogue, and more artists. A few motor vehicles, permitted somewhat reluctantly on the island for absolutely necessary reasons, raise the dust of the narrow winding roads.

Monhegan is owned by about 160 people. Most of them are members of Monhegan Associates, a group founded by Theodore Edison (son of the late Thomas) and dedicated to preserving the natural wild beauty and desirable natural and historic features of the island. The year-round dwellers have always been edgy about invasions of their privacy and threats to the primeval character of their beloved island. Suggestions of change, usually labeled progress or convenience, are stonily and even stormily resisted. And rightly so. In no time at all it could become as much a tourist ruin as Martha's Vineyard and Cape Cod.

Five years ago Monhegan's significance in American history led to its designation as one of fourteen sites in twelve states to become national landmarks. In all of the United States only fifty-four such sites are officially registered by the Department of the Interior, and their integrity protected. Monhegan's residents—a total of forty-seven year round— now breathe easier.

I board with the Henley Days when I visit Monhegan. June Day was born on the island. She could write a book about it and perhaps some day she will. The island's world passes by her door and she misses none of it. June is a bright, good-looking woman and she'll be just as bright and good-looking when she's ninety.

June and I are having a cup of tea. She's just shipped her son, Courtney, off to the schoolhouse. Henley's out back fussing with the well, readying it for winter. I try to kid

HENLEY DAY

June about the book she should write. She tells me her father's the one who could have written it. Cass Brackett was his name. He had put down all the stories about Monhegan but never got around to showing them to anyone. Then he died and a daughter has all the stories stashed away but won't release them because of their salty character.

Henley appears. The well is all set. Henley is a powerful man of peaceful mien. He can be lobsterman, lighthouse keeper, general handyman, critic or philosopher, depending on the season and availability of work. His thoughts run deep. He chooses his words carefully. He calls the island "*Mun*higgin" and tells me he's lived on it most of his life. He tried the mainland once, some time back, but gave it up and returned to the island. "A man gets by with less here. He don't need an auto or a fancy wardrobe. And he's free of responsibilities for all those possessions. And free of the pressures of shoreside living."

"Islands have pressures," I say.

"Not so much. In cities when people want spiritual comfort they flock to churches and psychiatrists and have to pay high for it. Here you pray when you want, where you want, in solitude. You're free. And you're handsomely rewarded" — he gestured with a sweep of his big rough hand — "wherever you turn."

I tell him an island's surrounded by water. He's really trapped, living on an island. He's not free at all.

Henley thinks about that for a while. A long while. Then a slow smile. A sweet look of understanding fills his eyes. "That's on the outside," he says.

"Take mushrooms," says Slagboom.

We are sitting in June Day's front room. The morning is sunny. A small fire idles in the ashes of the fireplace. A lobster boat glides out of the channel headed for the open sea. Teco Slagboom is an exotic, remarkable and rare as the fascinating *Basidiomycetes* he stalks. Can one resist a delicious shudder at names like Death Cup or Destroying Angel? "They're all here," Teco says, "in these woods. But rare, not everywhere on the island. Of course we've edible varieties as well. There's chanterelle, coral, the oyster mushroom, boletus." He frowns. "Boletus is chancy, though, when eaten raw. It may be poisonous — or may not be."

Teco is trim, urbane, articulate. He was born in Surabaya in Dutch Java. He lives on Monhegan in the summer, shuttling to British Columbia for the winter. He is painter, botanist, gardener. Thirty-four years of his life have been devoted to these pursuits.

Teco keeps a peacock in his shower. The bird came from the kingdom of Swat, he explains blandly, partly by bus. He recalls a sea anemone named "Jezebel" who was fed too much raw hamburger and went into convulsions; and a Cecropia moth who laid eggs all over the drapes and hatched a studio full of caterpillars. Teco is rarely bored. Sometimes he runs sea urchin races on his kitchen table.

He admits that it's something of a sacrifice, giving up the mainland for so long a time. "But I'm a woods person and I'm attracted to Monhegan because it's a small, geological, physical island. Everything I want to paint, study and explore is within easy reach."

For a man who served his apprenticeship in a textile design studio, Teco's knowledge of flora and fauna is impressive. He speaks of the frogs that inhabited Monhegan ages past, when the sea level was three hundred feet lower. He talks with authority of the state program for "harvesting" the deer herd and "planting" pheasants. He knows of deep cover where woodcock nest and where the poisonous hemlock grows.

"Would you believe orchids on Monhegan?"

I nod. I would believe unborn palm trees in Alaska if Slagboom said so. "Fringed orchids," he goes on, his eyes gleaming. "And Texas bluebonnet in the wild state, from which the Russell lupine was hybridized. Escapees from seashore gardens."

It is too much. I am in over my head. "What about predators?" I ask in a low hoarse voice.

"The peregrine falcon," says Teco instantly. "The sharp-shinned hawk. The osprey. The marsh hawk. Clever, they are. They follow the flickers. Cedar waxwings line up on branches of spikenard and pass the berries down the line to one another. It's then the peregrine falcon swoops."

"Any other dangers I should look out for?"

"The poisonous berry of the deadly nightshade." He smiles. "Empty beer cans, candy wrappers . . ."

Teco Slagboom admits he could no longer stay year round on Monhegan, much as he loves it. He feels one has to have been brought up on the island to spend all of one's life on it. "You need an almost superhuman discipline," he explains sadly. "And, of course, a job."

Monhegan's harbor, between the main island and Manana Island, is deceptively peaceful-looking. In a southeast gale, a smashing surf piles in through the passage, often leaving disaster and tragedy in its wake. In one such night of rain, wind and pitch darkness in 1858, everything anchored in the strait, including fourteen fishing boats, was swept to total wreckage on the lethal black ledge of Smutty Nose. Just a couple of years ago, a chartered pleasure yacht dropped anchor at night to ride out the storm and was carried to sea. Bits of its wreckage, found much later, were all that remained to tell a story.

Manana (once known as Menana and Monanis) is occupied by the Coast Guard Station and an affable shepherd, a hermit named Ray Phillips. Phillips came to Manana years ago as a young man, choosing the solitary life over the big city rat race. I am unable to find Phillips. I inquire and Chris Nicholson tells me he's making one of his rare trips to the mainland to spend his money.

"He gets a veteran's pension and Social Security," Chris confides. "It kind of piles up on him."

Chris has been lobstering, fishing and running the mail since 1919, but is retired now. I ask him about Monhegan's unique lobstering law, which limits the local fishing to the first six months of the year.

"The way I see it," Chris tells me, "they couldn't make a living here lobstering the year round. You catch the biggest part of your lobsters on the cheapest price of the year. Now this way, you catch just as many lobsters, probably you catch more. And you get them at their best price. Well, I say the best price, but we used to get more. But you do get the lobster at his peak. He's filled out, see? His shell is hard when we catch him. Fishing year round, most of your lobsters is caught right after they've shed and they're soft. They haven't filled out and haven't got their shell full of meat. But they weigh practically the same 'cause where there's not meat, there's water."

"Most people who eat lobster don't know about that."

"Same way with us. When we eat a piece of beef, we don't have much idea how it's raised, do we? Same with our chickens today. Now they force them so hard, you know, they claim there's an awful lot of cancer, driving them so hard. And of course you know they never get on the ground. They never get outdoors."

June Day joins us about this time. It's a lovely autumn day. An army of tourists had come to the island on the morning mail boat from Port Clyde. June tells us they're artists and bird watchers. They stay at The Trailing Yew, which is the only place serving meals this time of year. "There's no sign of them in the winter," she sniffs.

I ask Chris and June about ice cutting. I read somewhere that it was an important part of the winter routine. Twenty years ago, the men on Monhegan cut and stored 275 tons of ice, cut from Monhegan's ice pond, mostly to preserve the fish catch. When gas refrigeration became available, the demand for natural ice diminished. Today, about sixty tons are cut by the Crystal Ice Company, and used mostly for iced drinks on the verandahs of the summer people. "We had beautiful ice last year," Chris says. "No snow in it."

Electric power is limited on Monhegan. People who want it have their own generators. I asked June if the island will ever have a power plant.

"The trouble is, we don't have the people. If you had the winter population as much as you have it in the summer, a power plant would support itself. But there's nothing but a handful of year-round people here and it's pretty expensive and won't support it."

"How many live here through the winter?"

"Forty-seven."

"What happens if you get sick or hurt in some accident?"

"If it's something *really* serious, you go to the mainland."

"I been a good many years here on the island," says Chris. "They all doctored themselves. I remember when automobiles first come in, I was out on Block Island then. You know, a kid will pick up things much easier and quicker than an older person, and I was driving this Model T car for this doctor and he says to me one time, him and I was sitting there alone in the office and he says, 'You see this big office and how I have a lot of office calls? Well,' he says, 'if I told 'em to go home and take a good dose of physic, I'd be out of business.' That was practically all your office calls. He was a good doctor, too."

JOURNAL NOTE: Jim Swihart is a Casco town selectman who spent most of his childhood summers on Chebeague Island in Casco Bay. He remembers a time when his maternal grandmother had just arrived for a long visit and received word to rush back to Indiana, where a close relative lay dying. Mrs. Swihart called in her son.

"Jimmy," she said, "you run down to Leonard's store and tell Mr. Leonard I want four hundred dollars. Hurry now."

To a six-year-old in 1921 four hundred dollars was as meaningless as a million. But he sensed the urgency in his mother's voice. It was a mile and a half to the general store and Jim ran all the way. He found Mr. Leonard in the store but he could not find the words. The old man leaned over the counter.

"The usual penny candy, Jimmy?"

Jimmy was still gasping for breath.

"What is it you want, Jimmy?"

"My mother—said to ask you—for four hundred dollars."

Mr. Leonard opened the cash drawer and cleaned it out of bills and went out back and got some more.

"There you are, Jimmy. Four hundred dollars."

That was all. That's how things were on Chebeague in 1921.

In the early morning before my departure from Monhegan I headed for the Cathedral Woods and whatever lay beyond. My mind dwelled on the berries of the deadly nightshade, Teco's poisonous hemlock and the fierceness of the peregrine falcon. I climbed the road past the abandoned lighthouse and looking back from the rise could see the trim shapes of lobster boats and small craft anchored in the harbor between Manana and Smutty Nose on one side and the pier and bathing beach on the other. They looked like old toys in a bathtub.

The narrow path led through stately woods carpeted in thick fern and pine needles. Except for a humming of insects, a deep silence lay over everything. The air was sharp and clean-smelling. I stopped to search a tree trunk's ground cover and froze. A movement in the woods nearby caught the corner of my eye. Very slowly I turned to look.

A deer, not thirty yards distant, was watching me. I have surprised deer before. They take off instantly and in moments are gone from sight. This one never moved. He was a buck with a splendid rack, a deep chest, snowy white, all of him in full prime. His flag was up and twitching. He was close enough for me to see his nostrils quivering. I expected him to leap away as each second passed. We remained like that, unmoving, for almost half a minute. Then he bounded off and was gone.

Why had he waited so long? Where had his fear of the two-legged stalker with the explosion stick gone? Hunting is forbidden on Monhegan. Had this creature come round to trust and faith in the absence of killing? Had he come round to the absence of fear?

Climbing over smooth granite I came out of the woods into the open cap of Black

Head rising upward from the ocean 150 feet in a sheer creviced naked wall. Wildflowers grow in profusion here. A proper place. People have slipped or been swept over its edge by high winds.

I could hear the sea smashing against the rocks below. Except for its rhythmic thunder, all silence. I was drawn to the edge, by what, I do not know. I peered as far over as I dared. Lobster buoys tossed on the wild surface close to the half-submerged rocks round which the sea roiled. Whose buoys were they? Which of the island lobstermen so defiantly courted disaster? Why? And what had drawn *me* so close? Only sky was there and sea below. I had never before felt so alone, confronted not only by the elements, but by my own life.

The sky darkened. I drew back. It was an effort. I hurried down the path through the Cathedral Woods. No deer now. A dampness, more foggy mist than rain, had settled on the leaves and grass. The sweat on my face and body felt clammy and cold. In the hush of things I brooded on the spell of this enchanted island. Why had the deer lingered? Why were the buoys set so dangerously close to the rocks? Had people at the cliff's edge slipped or been swept to death by the wind? Had they jumped or been pushed? I broke into a run.

The ferry had unloaded its cargo and passengers when I arrived at the dock. I climbed aboard. It was marvelous hearing people's laughter and merry voices in greeting and farewell. Forty-seven souls year round must get to know each other, trust each other, need each other, while summer people merely come and go. People are to love, I thought. Of all afflictions of the human heart, loneliness is the bitterest.

What's in store for Maine's offshore islands?

For generations Maine people have taken the land for granted. It never seemed valuable for anything but what they grew or grazed on it, or for the timber it yielded. The acreage and buildings passed down from generation to generation with little noticeable change except for the slow deterioration of the buildings and the mutilation of the surrounding woods. No one ever thought of it as real estate.

Now with the outward thrust of urban people to the country, a Maine land boom is on and there is cause for concern. Since World War Two, a number of land developers whose only purpose was quick profit moved in, bought cheaply, partitioned the land and moved out rich. In their wake they left sanitation problems, unfulfilled promises of recreational and transportation facilities and other public services, and a hundred headaches over schooling, local taxes, pollution and overcrowding.

Maine's islands offer a particularly tempting target to people who decide to get away from it all. To own an island is a status symbol loftier by far than His and Her Cadillacs. Islands are naturally attractive to people with boats, who use them for domiciles or pleasure and often for business and a tax write-off. But islands are becoming harder to find, increasingly costly and less accessible than before. Private Property signs, seawalls, chain link fences and visible pollution are some of the deterrents a sailor encounters these days.

One of the first steps to correct the deteriorating situation was a proposal in 1967 by the Department of the Interior through its Bureau of Outdoor Recreation, to form an island trust for the 324 islands comprising the Casco Bay group. The purpose of the trust was to protect the islands from commercial or industrial development, save the scenery, preserve historical landmarks and provide some environment for public enjoyment. Island areas in other states were included in the concept. In Maine, besides the Casco Bay group, trusts were suggested for Acadia National Park, Boothbay Harbor, the Muscongus Bay Islands (including Monhegan), the Penobscot Bay group and those along the upper east coast — more than 200,000 acres, excluding Acadia. And with the others across the nation, a total of 26,235 islands of ten acres or more for sensible public use and not for exploitation. Even recognizing the public's propensity for slothful desecration, it seemed a noble concept.

Where is it today? Nowhere. No federal legislation passed. No presidential order issued. But the outlook is not entirely bleak. A private group has been at work. It's called the Maine Coast Heritage Trust, with Elmer Beal, Jr., a descendant of a distinguished lobstering family, as its executive director. Headquarters are located on Mount Desert Island. Its purpose is to implement a new easement law which gives coastal and island property owners a voice in how scenic and environmental values should be preserved. It provides a hopeful solution to the problems of car graveyards, factories, oil refineries, or anything else the landowner might regard as threatening to the esthetic environment in which he lives.

Since 1963, another private group, the Maine chapter of The Nature Conservancy, has assisted in protecting twenty-three Maine islands or portions of islands, from the risk of commercial development. The Charles A. Lindbergs gave Big Garden Island, southwest of Vinalhaven to the Conservancy. Garrison Norton, a former Secretary of the Navy, donated Mark Island in West Penobscot Bay in memory of his son. Dram Island in Sorrento Harbor was swapped for a church organ. Many other islands vulnerable to exploitation will be preserved forever through the good work of the Conservancy.

27

LIFE IN
A SEACOAST VILLAGE

The mail boat to Monhegan Island departs each morning from her wharf in Port Clyde at ten-thirty. She's the *Laura B.*, skippered by Earl Fields, Jr., who took over the helm when his father retired. The passengers may be islanders, day tourists or week- to summer-long vacationers. Even more mixed is the cargo she carries—split firewood, a water pump, lobstermen's gear, luggage, cases of groceries, beer and wine for the Odom's store—one never knows what to expect. There follows quite a business of lashing down the cargo, covering it with tarps, and trusting it not to shift during the crossing. Which it invariably does.

Missing the mail boat is an occasional tourist hazard around Port Clyde. The less adventuresome latecomer stranded in this bare-bone seacoast village will find almost nothing to do except return to Thomaston. There is no cinema or saloon. The library hasn't opened for years. There won't be another boat until morning. But there's more to Port Clyde than meets the eye. The best thing to do is to check into Alma Heal's New Ocean House.

Alma Heal is a down-to-earth duchess in firm command of her fief. She rules the New Ocean House, an old-fashioned and comfortably sagging hostelry, with the aplomb of the professional and a faint touch of noblesse oblige. The structure was originally a sail loft and for the next hundred years or so, a lodging house. It seems not to have changed much. Alma's father, Fred Seavey, owned it and when he died Alma took over for her mother.

Alma is sixtyish, dry-witted and laconic. She's been on the go all of her life, working out of a wheelchair. When the Port Clyde water district was set up in 1966, Alma was made a director and its treasurer. She's also served as town clerk and registrar of deeds. Not bad for a country gal stricken with polio in 1924. "Judas Priest," she exclaims, "to this day I don't know how I do it." Nor does anyone else.

Alma holds court from her perch behind a huge desk in a room that's a reading room, office, candy store, hotel lobby and whatever else you want it to be when you're in it. She

is surrounded by an imposing array of letters and postcards, account books, old magazines and small articles for sale. A random library of romantic novels written at the turn of the century molders on two bookshelves that have the impromptu look of an afterthought.

The New Ocean House operates a gift shop on an unpublished schedule. One can purchase toothpaste, plastic hair combs, picture postcards and what is generally known in rural Maine as sundries. If you time it right and you're lucky, you'll find Charlene Coolbroth tending shop. Charlene is sixteen and attends Crosby Junior High when she isn't helping out at Alma's. Charlene's chores include bed making, house cleaning and, best of all, understudying Alma in her incredible kitchen.

Incredible indeed! The work/clean/eat/chat area resembles the movie set in that cramped ocean liner stateroom occupied by the four Marx brothers. Seated in the midst of an appalling assemblage of pots and pans, table and chairs, spice shelves and canned goods, Alma is in cool command, with her husband in quiet attendance. She confirms a reservation from a New Jersey couple for the weekend; instructs Charlene in the mysteries of seasoning the chowder; sells two ten-cent candy bars to a tow-headed barefoot youngster; plans the apple and blueberry pies for the evening meal; and soothes an arriving couple who are uneasy because there's no key to their upstairs room. "No use," Alma explains easily. "The doors just won't shut tight enough to lock 'em, anyway."

In a relaxed interlude, Alma speaks of the celebrities who have come and gone at the New Ocean House. Tom Dewey off a yacht. Bobby Kennedy off another yacht and playing touch football with a few chums on the hotel lawn. I'm startled by the casual phrasing. What lawn? The hotel has a parking lot on one side, the gift shop on the other, and its front piazza butts right into the road. And, oh yes, John Glenn and Andy Wyeth when he was a kid and Peter Hurd, the artist . . .

She rings up the candy sale on the combination McCaskey old model cash register-adding machine. I ask Alma why the doors to the hotel rooms don't shut properly. "It's built on ledge, is why," says Alma. "The floor frames heave in the changing season and the whole place settles in the oddest ways." The inn, she tells me, was one of the most notorious taverns on the coast, prior to and during Prohibition. A rumrunner's haven, the house is full of secret closets, dumbwaiters and hidden cellars. The chimney place in her bedroom has concealed shelves for bottled liquor. And there are shelves under the stairways for "Belgium alcohol." Whatever that means.

Does she get many permanent boarders? "Well," Alma says, "there was this one artist stayed a week. Got rained off Monhegan. Painted every view from every window. Ended up on the john painting his reflection in the mirror."

"What became of him?"

"Had a big exhibition in New York. The whole show was the views he painted from the New Ocean House. Sold out, so I'm told."

The décor of Alma Heal's New Ocean House is highly original. The dining room is dominant golden oak tastefully relieved by U.S. 1 bric-a-brac. Several paintings and prints donated by resident artists are remarkably competent. One aquarelle in particular, of Owl's Head Lighthouse, by Joseph Barber, catches the grace and strength of its subject's eminence, rooted in the rock of Port Clyde's shoreline. The furnishings in the upstairs bedrooms invoke memories of a summer weekend spent in Georgia in an atmosphere best described as Early Tufted Chenille Recherché.

Nothing really to see or do in Port Clyde. Heaven help the stranded tourist. The Hocking Bros. quarry is long gone. The cannery burned in October of seventy. And they say the lobstering and shrimping ain't what it used to be. But there's Alma's baked beans and blueberry pie and some of the freshest repartee this side of Artemus Ward. If you like that sort of thing. And I do.

N. C. Wyeth's summer home on Horse Point Road is still occupied at times by his widow, now in her eighties. The house is unusual in that it was floated to Port Clyde from Caldwell Island where, I'm told, there's buried treasure. The fish dock can be fascinating, expecially when the boys are weighing in their halibut catch. Then there are the lobster fishermen. Men like Charley Culver. His fish shack is hard by the public landing.

I stop by this late morning but Charley's boat is out. I decide to come back later. At the corner opposite the Dip Net, a snack bar, I find the Alvah Thompson house. George has already photographed the Thompsons. Alvah is "sick-a-bed" but I spend a few minutes chatting with Helen Thompson over coffee. The small parlor is brightly papered, cluttered with family memorabilia of half a century. I inquire about the photograph of a salty-looking man in a navy uniform. It's Helen's brother. "He was in the Coast Guard," she tells me, "and stationed on that island out there and when he was retired he moved out there and he's living there right now."

She has a granddaughter living in Rockville, Connecticut, and a son who lives between Port Clyde and Tenant's Harbor. "Everybody calls him Cappy. He's a whiz on outboards and, well, any kind of motor, come to think of it."

I ask her if it's a nuisance in the summer, all those cars and people coming and going to the Monhegan ferry.

"Oh, it's interesting. Too interesting maybe, because there's so many people, you can't get around. They come for a look at Monhegan. Just curious, you know, and of course everybody that goes down there likes it and they stay as long as they can. I lived on Monhegan one winter. My husband went lobstering down there. Then we come back and lived over there on that island."

She points across the open bay. "Hooper Island, it's called. Beautiful over there, but, you know, it isn't an island any more. It's a city. They have electric lights. Artesian wells. When I lived there, we had cattle. Oxen did the work."

"How'd you get back and forth?"

"We rowed. Then we got a little outboard like they use now. That was great. A seven and a half horsepower, it was. That was 1936. We lived on Hooper Island from 1919 to

1936. My oldest girl went to school from there with other children who lived there. We'd bring 'em over in the morning and came and got 'em in the afternoon. They had a good time."

"Did you know the N. C. Wyeths when they lived here?"

"Oh yes. Our place on the island was right across from their place. Right across the harbor. He's dead, you know. But my son's wife worked for her this summer. She doesn't come too often now. It's a beautiful place up there. Lovely piazza to sit on. And of course we all know Andy. And his boy Jamie. I hear they have a nice place down there to Monhegan. I haven't been there for years. Every year I say I'm going, but then the crowd starts gathering and I say that's no place for me. I'd love to go down some time and visit the gift shops. They say they're really nice. But all the people I knew are gone."

I tell Mrs. Thompson I'm staying at Alma Heal's New Ocean House.

"It used to be just the Ocean House," she explains. "The post office used to be down in the store and Alma's father was the postmaster and they lived upstairs. Had a store there. She got infantile and she's been in the wheel chair since. She has a son and he's the superintendent of schools. Lionel."

Helen Thompson describes what it was like a year ago that September, when the sardine cannery burned down. "That was a horrible fire. If the wind had been out that way, it would have cleaned all the houses up there on the hill."

I ask her if that's where Bill Thon, the painter, lives. I'm planning to visit him next. It is, and Mrs. Thompson tells me the Thons have been coming to Port Clyde for years, even before they built their house. "They travel a lot, him and his wife Helen. Florida, Italy . . ."

Is Port Clyde changed much from the old days? She thinks it's about the same. "'Course there's a lot of new people have come in and a lot of cottages have gone up. There's twenty-two cottages on that island that's gone up since we left there."

They left in 1936. Twenty-two cottages in thirty-five years isn't exactly a building boom, but this is Maine and an island. I ask her how she feels about all that activity.

"It's all right with me. Live and let live."

"And Mr. Thompson?"

"Feels the same. He likes all the people over there. Stopped over a while back and had a chat with them and we liked 'em all. Most of 'em are from Massachusetts."

Alvah Thompson's given up lobstering. "He's eighty-six now," his wife tells me. "He put out his traps this spring but he had to give it up. So he gave them to my grandson. Now, his birthday was the ninth of September and he got up and we had cake and ice cream. All the family was here and he had a great time. Then my birthday was the twenty-ninth and my niece came over from Vinalhaven and visited me and we had another nice time. He was up and again he had his ice cream and cake. But I notice soon's he gets up he's always nauseated and has to go right back to bed. The doctor says it's just old age. That man hasn't got an ache nor a pain. He's just given up. He says when he can't work, he doesn't want to live. 'Cause he's always gone lobstering. It's been his whole life ever since he was a little boy. Used a dory, you know. Had no boat engines then. Him and his brother, they used to go together. He was twelve or thirteen then. They used to go after sea birds. They shot a hole right out through the bow of the dory one day. They couldn't swim, not one of them, and they was overboard. They made it back all right. Now, my oldest son, when we lived over there on the island, he couldn't swim. But he got a girl friend and he went to visit her and he learned to swim in a darn old quarry. If I'd a known that, I'd a had a fit. It's stagnant. Isn't fit to go in. Now, with all this nice water around, he had to go swimming in there."

"Why'd you move off the island?"

"Why, my older girl got to be ten and then we had two more children and there was nobody over there to go to school, so we had to move over here. And we had an old schoolhouse up here, an old rickety thing that my children went to. Then they built a beautiful schoolhouse, water and flush toilets, and how long did we have it? No time at all. They put a bulldozer in it and tore it down. Pathetic. To put a road through. It was right up there on the corner, right where you go on the new road. It sat right there. When I stop and think of that old schoolhouse that my children went to and then they build something like that and tear it down. Then these little kids that should be home, have to get on a school bus and go over to Tenant's Harbor and stay all day long. And it's just the same everywhere, busing schoolchildren. I think it's a shame.

I ask Mrs. Thompson if she ever thought of living somewhere else.

"Well now, I'll tell you." She nods toward the bedroom. "He said we can't keep this place on our hands no longer and I'm trying to sell it. Put the right people in here, you could get sixty-five dollars a month rent. A nice apartment on the other side, another one downstairs. The post office used to be down here years ago. There isn't too much land, just the land around the house itself. I thought if I could sell it, I'd get us a trailer. My son has plenty of land and he wants us to come over there and then he could look after us, hook up the water at his well. They've got a lovely well."

"And that's where you'd settle down?"

"That's where. He's sick and it doesn't make much difference. 'Course he wouldn't want to leave this place, but those stairs get to you after a while. And we've got to have all new stairs. My son came down the other day and went right through a board. Everything's gone, so we've got to have everything new."

"What was your family name?"

"Knowlton. My father came from way up in the country, way up in Belmont, Belfast way, and my mother came from Vinalhaven. My father went over there to preach and that's where they met. And my grandma run a boarding house over there. Course that was before my time but they used to cut granite over there. That was a big busy place, Vinalhaven. It's a beautiful spot. There's a lovely ferry that goes over there and you can take your car. I think it cost you fifteen dollars over and back. But in the summertime, is that booming! My heavens!"

I get up to leave and express my hopes for Alvah's speedy recovery.

She shrugs. "Well, yesterday he was up and sat up all the afternoon, but today—he tumbled. He's fallen down twice. I have all I can do to get him up. He's weak and the longer you lay in bed the weaker you're going to get. He's had a hard life."

"If he had it to do over again, do you think he'd pick lobstering?"

"He certainly would. It's what he knows best and he wouldn't do anything else."

AUTHOR'S NOTE: On April 26, 1972, Mrs. Alvah (Helen A.) Thompson wrote: "My husband passed away March 6 after a winter of being very sick. I am very lonesome still here in the big old house, have a chance to sell but very undecided, it's an awful decision to have to make after all these years."

Mrs. Thompson pointed the way to Bill Thon's place. George joined me and we followed the road to a low, handsome structure in a secluded woodland setting with a lovely view of the sea. I had never met Bill Thon but I'm familiar with his work. It's much better known in New York, Paris and London than it is in Maine. We are made welcome. I study his canvasses, several of which are hung around the house. Thon paintings hang in homes, museums and galleries round the world.

Bill Thon paints delicate, compellingly lovely landscapes executed in a highly original style. He is pretty much self-taught. His only formal training consisted of one unhappy month at the Art Students League, which he felt "wasn't for him."

On his own, he worked a long and hard apprenticeship in commercial art studios doing displays for drugstores, posters and color layouts and whatever else came across his drawing board in the busy bullpens of Madison Avenue. But he hungered for a change.

"I was born in lower Manhattan's Hell's Kitchen," he explains. "But I grew up on sand beach and loved it. I decided a long time ago I wanted a shore with woods down to the sea."

Bill Thon married Helen Walters in 1929. They made trips to Maine whenever they could get away. It wasn't until his navy World War II service was over that they began to look in earnest for the place they wanted. He discovered the rocky, woodland shore setting around Port Clyde, bought a piece of land and built a little camp to live in.

Stone by stone, timber by timber, the Thons put together a remarkable home, using materials harmonious with their tastes and designing the structure both inside and out to accommodate their particular living style.

We sit with Helen and Bill Thon surrounded by their handiwork. Gleaming wood, smooth stone, handsome furniture, the folds of finely textured fabric. Everything they have made here creates a serene setting for his paintings. Bill is telling us in his soft, reserved way about his boat. He works hard and best in the winter, from Labor Day to April. But as soon as the ice is out, he readies *Echo,* his Friendship sloop (Registry #54, Friendship Sloop Society), built by Lee Boatyard of Rockland. A twenty-two-footer, she won the Lash Brothers Trophy in the 1969 races.

I watch his strong-fingered craftsman hands as he speaks. Sure and reliable, I think, at an easel, a helm or a power saw. I think of his paintings, world travelers to far-off places. Does he miss them like distant children?

Later, driving back to Alma Heal's, I review my notes and thoughts. The most lasting impression of the Thons is the quality of serenity and accomplishment I found there. The Thons have a good life, I tell myself. It comes in the sharing of hardships and setbacks. It comes in taking the good and the bad in stride. What matters most is that both take it equally and together. And out of it must come something worthwhile and lasting—like the art of William Thon.

We drive past the burned-out shell of the sardine factory. It still smells faintly of char.

I figure it's time to catch up with Charley Culver now, and I head down to the harbor.

Charley Culver came out of Cape Charles, Virginia, to serve with the Coast Guard on Burnt Island in 1955. He liked it and stayed. For about ten years he fished out of a second-hand Boudreau-built lobster boat with Johnny Hupper and then went off on his own. He fishes year round, setting as many as 425 traps, handling half of them every day, spring, summer and fall.

In the wintertime he hauls as much as 1,500 pounds of fresh fish and seafood to Route 202, his regular stand in Parsippany near Morristown, New Jersey. He picks up the shrimp and lobster around Port Clyde and the fresh catch of flounder, sole, halibut and cod on the Portland fish wharves.

Charley and his raw-boned, red-bearded helper are in Charley's fish shack talking with George and me. We're drinking beer because the evening is hot and we're dry as dust. Mentioning cod reminds me of a fish market in Rockland where they sell cod tongues and cheeks. I ask a landlubber's question: "What're they like and who buys them?"

The helper's eyes gleam. "Delicious. Best eatin' part of the cod. But most outsiders, they won't touch it."

He sails his empty beer can into the trash drum and peels open another. Charley is fussing with a length of snarled line. They had a fair day outside but he seems grumpy. The summer fishermen are getting into his hair, he says. As many as eighty of them with lobstering licenses right now, compared to ten or fifteen in the rugged winter months. At least there's an unwritten agreement that holds them in line. *Fish your own back yard or lose your traps.*

Charley drags on his cigarette, runs strong fingers through his thatch of dark hair. "Lobstering ain't what it used to be," he says. I want to laugh because he's young and cannot possibly know what it "used to be" for lobstermen like Dennis Eaton and Alvah Thompson. Or Gooden Grant of Stonington, who lobstered alone out of Head Harbor on Isle au Haut until he was eighty-four, more than a dozen years ago. Or "Henry" Watson out of Friendship, past ninety now and blind, who started at twelve and got a nickel a pound for his lobster catch.

"Ninety cents for shedders," Charley grunts, "and a buck forty or fifty for keepers."

The overhead is draped with Charley's gaudy buoys. Gaudy is good. You can spot them easier in thick fog and a dirty sea. The shack is too warm and smells of cordage and paint, spilled beer and male sweat. I'm trying to remember what it is that makes shedders cheaper than keepers, whether the average buyer knows the difference or gives a damn.

I check the time. It's past the supper hour and there's half a dozen cans of cold beer unpeeled. I've had all the beer I can hold. I walk outside to relieve myself. A long unsteady look at Port Clyde harbor in moonlight transforms it into Cannes and Hong Kong and Nassau. Lighted decks and clean boat shapes and the warm embrace of sheltering hills. The air is heavy and sweet. Somewhere a pump clanks faintly. Shedders or keepers. It boggles the mind.

I bid the boys a loud good night. Up the hill and round the bend the road curves past trim frame cottages built small to hold the heat snug against winter. Familiar rock floats from their wallpapered innards, mixed with the shrill pleas of too familiar TV pitch talk. Past the locked darkened general store spruce green in cloudy moonlight, past the Dip Net and the stiff façade of neglected Hutler's. The kitchen light in kindly Mrs. Thompson's upstairs place reminds me of her patient, lonely vigil.

The ribbed boat landing sucks in the lacy edges of the sea. My last look is into the harbor. Shadowy hulls ride a cleansing southwest wind with the grace of resting gulls. I pass the parking lot where touring seafarers to Monhegan leave their locked cars overnight. A cooling finger of wind, light as down, strokes my cheek. A minute more and I'm at the front door of the New Ocean House, Alma Heal, Prop.

Shedders or keepers? I fall into my cave of a bed and in instant sleep dream of Bookbinders Sea Food House in Philadelphia, final resting place of the best of the keepers.

JOURNAL NOTE: Through the lean winter to the rawness of April, town women young and old work in the local shrimp processing plant. Many of them do it to earn the six hundred dollars it takes to qualify them for unemployment relief, but they all need the money for one thing or another. It's day or night work depending on when the shrimp draggers bring in their catch. The pay is minimal and working conditions far from ideal.

The women stand (no sitting is permitted) and strip the pink shrimp flesh from the shells along a moving belt. They discard the residue, spilling legs and tails and the heads with their beadlike black eyes into a trough of flowing icy green seawater.

The young ones, many of them high school girls, detest the job; the older ones accept it as part of the hard life they lead. The eight-hour night shift quits at midnight. Outside the temperature is well below freezing and the world smells of shrimp.

46

CREATIVE PEOPLE

Winslow Homer at Prout's Neck. Rockwell Kent on Monhegan. John Marin at Small Point. William Zorach at Robinhood. Whatever the magic in seacoast Maine, it worked remarkably well down the years for these celebrated artists. It works just as well today for Andrew Wyeth at Cushing and Clark FitzGerald at Castine. It works for the hundreds of creative people in the visual and performing arts who live year round or come to Maine each year; it provides a source of inspiration, a rejuvenation of the artistic spirit.

Just exactly why this is so, no one can truthfully say. There are prettier places, more easily accessible, offering a variety of tempting creature comforts. Yet artists in increasing numbers choose Maine. Maine has *something*—in the character of its plain durable people, in the challenge of its harsh life style, in the raw rugged nature of the land—that draws the artist to it, a catalyst to his creativity. For Homer it was his fascination with man's physical and spiritual struggle against the elements. For Zorach, a tactile infatuation with the gentler forms of nature surrounding him.

Serious artists are reluctant to talk about their work. The work must speak for itself. Yet those I visited were quite willing to express their personal feelings about Maine and how Maine affects their work. Some conversations and correspondence were nostalgic, like the ones with Peggy Bacon and Sally Avery. Some veered toward the technical and professional, like the one with Jamie Wyeth. In all of my conversations with Maine artists I was aware of a *simpatico* that exists, as it does nowhere else I know of in America, between the artist and his chosen sanctuary of inspiration.

In her valuable work *Maine, A Guide "Down East,"* Dorris Isaacson tells us, "The greatest concentration of artistic activity early in the Twentieth Century was at Monhegan." Today it is everywhere along the coast and inland. Summer art galleries are finding it profitable to stay open year round. Inland towns like Naples, Norway and Bridgton in the Sebago-Long Lake region, hold annual arts festivals that attract summer people from all over New England.

To include here all the talented artists and craftsmen who work year round in Maine becomes an impossible task. I've talked with a few I know or have met or simply stumbled on by chance. Year round or transient, native or alien, they are truly creative people, each in his chosen field. When they speak of Maine and why they are here and what it is they do, I feel they speak for all the others.

I'm on the Pemaquid road in morning sunlight. My thoughts dig into a dimmer past. I have not been down this elongated finger of Maine in many years. Memories come spilling back like dust motes, back to a time when Sally and Milton Avery spent a painting summer on Pemaquid Point.

Milton's gone now, a gentle, handsome man whose work was his life. His paintings hang in important museums and private collections and today are more cherished, more sought after, than he could possibly have dreamed they would be while he created them. Much of Avery's strength and beauty, according to one art critic, comes from his uniting of at least two major traditions of the past—French Impressionism and Cubism.

The beauty of Avery—yes, perhaps. But his greatest source of strength? Sally. Only Sally. She believed steadfastly in Milton's art. She subordinated (but did not sacrifice) her own ambitions as a painter to free Milton from the role of breadwinner and from any other distractions that might hinder his single-minded absorption with his painting. As Sally Michel, she worked through the Depression and the war years as a free-lance commercial artist in New York's hectic fashion world, picking up assignments at department stores and ad agencies, racing about Manhattan breathless and harried, yet always full of wit and cheer. Her pen-and-ink sketches were a regular and popular feature of the Sunday *New York Times Magazine* children's page.

During those rare summer days at Pemaquid, Sally relaxed from the rat race of business and painted to her heart's content. I remember only pure delight, all of us sprawled across the slippery, canted face of Pemaquid Point, sketching and laughing and the sea below hurling itself against the rocks and the city remoter than the moon.

I wrote to Sally, eager to have her reflections about those days at Pemaquid. She wrote back:

We rented a house in Pemaquid in 1949 because one of our friends, Willard Macgregor, had been going there for years. The house was small and ugly and had 12 clocks which chimed every 15 minutes. The first night we almost went crazy. We were a few hundred yards from the rocky coast where we went every afternoon to sun and sketch. Mornings we worked on watercolors, using the porch as studio and usually wrapped in wool scarfs to ward off the foggy wind. We fixed up a badminton court on the lawn which effectively ruined the lawn but we had fun. Evenings we played charades or read poetry or wandered down to Willard's who would play Mozart for us. And so went the summer.

Our Vermont place you saw was in Rawsunville, about 13 miles from Manchester.

We rented a cat for the summer for 25 cents. It was little and scrawny but blossomed into a long-haired beauty. We tramped the mountains for miles around sketching. And we went swimming in Salmon Hole where once the Indians had massacred the inhabitants. Just before we left, March [their daughter] contracted the mumps so we stayed on into October until she was well. Then we were enchanted by all the flaming beauty of the New England autumn.

In September 1971, the Avery Family exhibition of paintings was hung in the Allentown, Pennsylvania, Museum. Paintings by Milton, Sally and March Avery (now Mrs. Philip Cavanaugh), who was barely old enough to hold a brush that time in Pemaquid. In the catalogue introduction, Frank Getlein writes:

> That is why this exhibition is so beautifully appropriate, combining as it does the work of the master with that of his wife, Sally Michel Avery — who was for many years by far the better known of the pair — and that of their daughter, March Avery, who has been well received in exhibitions in many parts of the country. Inevitably, the visitor will make comparisons and note certain similarities among the three. But the real similarity is not the manner, but the source, a long life of mutual endeavor, achievement, respect and love.

Love is what it takes.

The sun is higher now. It's Gene Klebe I'm to visit this morning. "You'll see my name on the mailbox," he told me. The road uncoils. Ahead somewhere before Pemaquid is the South Bristol boatyard of Harvey Gamage, lover of boats, builder of wooden vessels; the last, perhaps, of Maine's master craftsmen. I speak later of Harvey Gamage and I still speak of love.

And here is Gene Klebe's mailbox.

What first attracted me to Gene Klebe's work was his damned virtuosity. Here were these watercolors of the sea and ships and navy men and lobster gear, splashy, still wet, full of the salty vigor of the sea, yet marvelously disciplined. The kind of absolute authority that drives a lesser talent out of his skull.

Klebe seems immune to error. Whether it's his training or his Pennsylvania German aplomb, it's a foolproof combination that ranks him among Maine's most distinguished and popular year-round artists. Much of his success stems, as it does with Jamie Wyeth, from total involvement since childhood. Klebe's never held a salaried job. All of his life he's made his own way as an artist.

"I'll tell you about the very first time I came here," he says. "I was a counselor at a camp and a friend of mine had a home up in Kent's Hill. So he said when the camp season is over, we'll go up there and I'll show you Maine. I had never been in Maine. This camp was in Pennsylvania and I lived in Philadelphia. This was while I was in school. So we came up and we took a picnic to Pemaquid Point and I was impressed. I said this is it. This is the spot I want to paint. You never can run out of subject matter. I still haven't. There's acres and acres of subject matter, actually.

"After Mary and I were married, we decided to come up for a summer vacation. We rented a cottage. Then we finally bought that cottage. Then we moved up here twenty-six years ago. This was a frontier area at that time. They're trying to keep it that way, but they didn't start early enough. As you come up Route 1, for instance, years ago around Portland there were the regular ways to get into town; the signs, the gas stations and all that business. Well, these things have gradually moved up this way. Along the roads, the woods have been cut back. Bulldozers have gone in and ruined the landscape. Then someone comes along and sets up some sort of eyesore, a cheese store or something like that, and it ruins the scenery."

"You put in some war service didn't you?"

"Just with the Navy. The things that I did are still actually secret. And I'm still involved with the Navy. In fact, next week I'm going down to the Grumman testing ground and they're going to test out the F-14 and I'm going to record their testing and do sketches, photographs and paintings. The F-14's a fighter plane and flies at about three times the speed of sound, so I hope I get a flight on that."

"Are you conscious of style when you paint?"

"Not at all. I have my own style, naturally. I really don't know my style until it's put to me by the people who buy the paintings. They say, well, we like your painting because it's not just surface scenery. They have a depth to them, they have a feeling that you interpret and it's the same feeling we have but we can't interpret it your way, except that it reminds us of Maine."

"Do you keep track of where your paintings are?"

"We try to. We were over in Europe in October and the ambassador, Watson in Paris, invited us for cocktails at the embassy residence. He showed us all around this beautiful castle-mansion they live in. He's a serious art collector and he has a lot of French paintings. 'Now I want to show you something,' he says. 'There are two Corots and there is a Monet and there is a Klebe.' I felt pretty good."

"How do you feel about Maine? Is it going to hell?"

"I think it'll preserve its life and enthusiasm and wilderness, even though at present a lot of people are really scared. I think it's a good thing they're scared, I think that's what will save it."

"Zoning is what most towns need, isn't it?"

"Sure. But resistance to zoning is this so-called 'independence' that many Maine natives have. They want to control their property and they don't want anybody to say what's to be done with it. I just feel that some of that is not independence as much as it is ignorance. Maine is changing. When we first moved here, you could go down to Portland or you could go away for the weekend and you didn't have to lock anything. Nobody would come

SEACOAST MAINE

in. When we went away recently we had two men who started a patrol business inspecting various places where people were away or checking cottages when they were away all winter. So we hired them and we also notified the sheriff. Nevertheless, we were very relieved and happy when we came home and saw that everything was as we left it."

Mary Klebe, who keeps busy being a successful painter's wife and running their antique business, joins the conversation. I ask her how the days pass.

"Too quickly. There are always things to be done. I do some of Gene's typing and things like that. I run the errands. In the summer, particularly, we have the antique shop and the gallery and it keeps me busy."

"Is the shop here?"

"Out in the barn. I do some shopping for antiques during the winter and try to do all the things we have to let go during the summer."

Gene says: "Mary's one of the directors of the Maine Antique Dealers Association."

"How many dealers are there?"

"I read somewhere there were about a hundred in the organization. I think there are more than that now. Maybe eight hundred antique dealers in the state of Maine."

"Must one be a dealer to belong?"

"In some form. You don't have to have a shop, but you have to be a licensed dealer. In order to get in, the board of directors sits and really takes you to pieces. They want to be sure the members are honest and reliable dealers. There have been quite a few that have applied but didn't get in, because they either had a shop with mixed gifts and antiques so the public didn't know what they were paying for, or there was some question about the integrity of the dealer."

"So I can expect integrity where a Maine Antique Dealers Association card or license is displayed."

"It's supposed to be like that. As the president says, there are always a few slipups now and then. But they do the best they can to have a very select group. There are plenty of other dealers that are very good too, but just don't bother to join. The ones that are members have been really screened."

Gene says: "Maine has so much that is typically Maine. Like lobster boats and lobster pots. Farm implements. I've done paintings of fishermen mending nets. I've done pictures of draggers with their nets dropped down. It's beautiful, especially when they're reflected in water."

"You feel Maine is unique in what it has, compared with the rest of the country?"

"Yes, I do. The people who come here, who have never been in Maine, have that surprise of never having seen anything like it before. Living here, we get used to it."

"Like Maine lobstermen?"

"And the scenery and whatnot. You wouldn't believe that working out there on the sea, a lobsterman would be interested in the scenery. I was over on Monhegan and I was out with a man named Davis, a quiet fellow, a lobsterman. He asked me about cameras. He said, 'You know, one of the summer people here told me what was a good camera to get. I want to take pictures because I get out here when people are still asleep. I get out here at dawn, alone on the sea, and I see these beautiful sights and I want to record them.' Now, that's unusual, isn't it? For just a worker, I mean."

"Maine people have a deep awareness of the beauty around them," I say, "but often are unable to express it in words."

"They have that sense," Gene says, "and you don't realize it until somebody speaks up, somebody like Davis. Maine people work hard and they're always busy, but they never miss what's going on around them at the same time."

JOURNAL NOTE: The wood ceilings of the open porches of Maine's white clapboard houses are always painted bright sky blue. I don't know why and can't seem to find out, but I don't intend to stop trying.

The road to Emily Muir's place on Indian Point Road curves like a sickle past a pond drenched green in lily pads. A swing to the right through deep young pine growth reveals glimpses of water and sky but no dwelling. Until you're there. Clean and friendly shapes of stone, wood and glass join granite ledge outcroppings framed by the sea and the outlying islands.

Emily Muir once lived on Bank Street in New York's Greenwich Village and studied at the Art Students League in New York. One of her teachers was the celebrated draughtsman Bridgman. "Not such a great guy," she reflects, recalling a Bridgman charcoal sketch with a left foot on a right leg.

She was married to the sculptor William Muir, whom she met at the League and who was a director of Deer Isle's Haystack Mountain School until his death in 1964.

She is a meticulous craftsman, a creator of beauty in lasting forms. She uses canvas, fabric, stone, sand, wood to express her artistic wishes. Her work is in numerous private collections as well as the Brooklyn Museum and several University of Maine collections. She is the author of *Small Potatoes,* a novel about the way life was when she first moved here.

Her studio home is itself a work of art. Each detail of design, functional or decorative, seems serene and lasting. I relax in the presence of choice materials worked lovingly. Through the windows to the east past a sinewy William Muir granite sculpture, I see the Deer Isle thoroughfare and Isle au Haut and I remember Dennis Eaton's sheep.

Emily Muir hasn't the faintest idea why I'm here. She is too well-mannered to ask outright. So I tell her. A matter of chance. And I'd been told about her houses.

"Oh," she says, brightening. "The houses."

"How many are there now?"

"Let me see—twenty new ones, and at least ten more extensively remodeled."

"Why'd you decide to design houses?"

She smiled. "You might say I'm a missionary at heart. I felt, in the old days around

here—you know, years ago, everyone had nice homes. I don't mean expensive ones. Even the smallest ones had a sense of proportion and workmanship. That was true through all of New England, as you probably know. Back two centuries ago, certainly, and up to the middle of the last century. And then people just began to build boxes. It kept bothering me, and I decided to do something about it."

"When'd you build the first one?"

"In 1959. Would you care to drive out and look at some of them?"

We drive out to the road, Emily telling me it isn't Indian Point, after all. That is just what some people began to call it. She always called it Clam City. "Actually, we live beyond Clam City. It might be called a suburb of Clam City."

Through the village and round the other side of the island, climbing steadily, it seems. The first development of Emily Muir's we visit is at Crockett Cove. Seven single residences, tucked out of sight at the lower cove, four at the upper. One more is still in the planning stages. We meet an out-of-town couple up for the weekend to check their house before their summer stay. They welcome Emily warmly. It's evident how much they admire her for who she is and for what she has done.

The remarkable thing about an Emily Muir house is its personality. No house is like another. Each is planned for optimum privacy, yet designed to take full advantage of the stunning water views provided by the contours of its location. Seen from the water, each dwelling seems to grow naturally out of ledge and forest, all of it and its setting joined to the sea.

Inside, one comes to realize the extent and depth of Emily Muir's enormous talent. Her jewel-like designs accent the rooms and passageways like the maker's mark on antique silver.

In this day of ticky-tacky and trailer living, the missionary zeal of an Emily Muir is noble. She could have built for profit, using the shoddy materials and high-powered promotional techniques of the developers who vandalize the natural beauty of our seacoast and lakes; but she is an artist, sensitive to her environment and incapable of molesting beauty in nature.

"Artists," she says, "are the true leaders of our times. They should inspire and not degrade. There is a difference between shocking us into recognition of a situation and leading us to despair."

Emily Muir goes her quiet way creating art that will survive for generations. What she is preserving is a priceless heritage. "After all," she says, "art at first was limited to the church, then the wealthy, and then it became pictures on a wall. Today it shows signs of becoming what it should be—a part of everything around us, our clothing, our homes, our cities, our very lives. Art should reflect the best of all these."

Denny Dietz paints. Her husband Lew writes. They live in a large cozy clapboard colonial with a stunning view of Rockport's jeweled harbor. Denny asks if I'd like to see her studio.

I would love to see her studio. We cross through kitchen and back hall to reach it. En route I congratulate her. A picture story on Maine's women artists ran a week or so ago in an edition of the *Maine Times*. Denny Winters, which is how she signs her paintings, had been featured in a two-page spread along with Jeanne Dale Bearce, Emery Goff, Beverly Hallam and Dahlov Ipcar. The photographs were by Ms. Pat Jones.

Denny's studio is an attractive clutter of canvas and frames, easels and paint-gobbed tables. Paintings line the walls and are stacked everywhere. The big room smells pleasantly of turps and oil and paint, of sprayed paper and gessoed linen, the way an honest working studio should smell.

Denny shows me around explaining where and when a work was done, but never why. I listen politely but my eyes search for a large beach scene that a week ago graced the exhibit at the Maine Coast Artists Gallery in Rockport. I spy it. It moves me as provocatively, as disturbingly, as before. It shows a young woman in a bikini, her face flushed, her eyes roguish. Denny caught her in a moment of dark musing and her secret smile defies the Mona Lisa's. Behind her the beach sand stretches to infinity.

Denny watches me and seems amused. I tell her how much I admire the work but I dare not ask her to explain the secret mischief in the young woman's mind. Perhaps I already know.

We look at drawings. Denny is wise, shy with strangers, deeply involved in her work. Years devoted to life studies have made her an enormously talented draughtsman. She creates the female form as men delight in observing it. Flawless, luminous, warmfleshed in cool shadows; enticing, never arrogant.

Lately she has been working in various media with abstract subject matter, using colorful, sweeping, restless forms. The compositions seem live and troubled. After a few minutes I too am troubled. War? Violence? Waste? What is Denny trying to tell us here? She is watching me. I shift about, finally confess to a preference for the representational work she does. My foot is now in my mouth but I plunge on. How can I not prefer these women she creates, to abstractions? They are as firmfleshed as Degas dancers, as comely as Renoir country maids. What I cannot understand, I tell her, is how a woman as womanly as she, can paint the female form with such outright male devotion.

She has the innate good grace to ignore my unwitting rudeness. "Devotion to beauty," she says, "isn't the prerogative of either one or the other of the sexes. All art begins with a love of the human form. I don't believe I could ever have sketched a tree if I had not first learned how to draw a nude well."

I mull over that. Denny excuses herself. She must look to the tea and goes off to the kitchen—itself a studio of the culinary art. I take a last look full of longing at the young woman on the beach. Will she still be there if I hurry? I curse myself. Never ask an artist *why*. Look and enjoy. That's why the painting's hung. To be enjoyed, not dissected.

I join Lew in the living room. Will I help him pull up the dory for the winter? We go outside. The sun sparkles and the air smells fresh of the sea. We descend a flight of stone steps imbedded in soft grassy earth. The dory rests on the pebbly beach, its season's work done. With neighborly help we raise her, flip her over and settle her in her winter berth on the seawall, half buried in a huge bush of wild asters. A neighbor asks, How come barnacles on one side of the hull and not the other? No one seems to know. I suggest right-wing barnacles. They're on the starboard side. Lew shakes his fine, shaggy head and we climb the stone steps to Denny's high tea.

I ask him about his friend the late Kosti Ruohomma. I knew Kosti Ruohomma only from photographs of his I had seen. His storm-lashed series on Monhegan Island for *National Geographic.* His nostalgic *Life* photo essay on the West Rockport one-room schoolhouse he went to as a kid. His shot of a train at dusk approaching Wiscasset station — a memorable and poignant farewell to the end of an era.

Kosti, an afflicted genius, died bedridden and paralyzed in 1961. He was only forty-seven. Like so many gifted artists, Kosti seemed relentlessly bent on his own destruction. He would take wild risks to get a picture exactly as he wanted it — or was that truly the reason? Was he perhaps challenging fate?

Lew speaks hesitantly of those years with Kosti Ruohomma. The memories are perhaps still painful. Lew wrote a touching article for *Down East* magazine about Kosti's photographs ". . . that reveal a love, a pain of parting, with a way of life that he saw slipping away."

Nor was Kosti without "this dark laughter." After long hours in his darkroom, ". . . loneliness would drive Kosti down from the hills like a hunting cat. If he found a friend out, his habit was to leave his calling card, a burnt-out flashbulb or an empty beer can. One day, not finding the Andy Wyeths at home, he carved on the dooryard pumpkin, 'Kosti was here.'"

The *Down East* piece is a fine example of heartfelt praise without mawkish sentimentality. It reflects Lew Dietz's depth of compassion and his scrupulous honesty as a reporter. A commemorative show of the best of Ruohomma's work, sponsored by the Maine State Commission on the Arts and the Humanities, recently traveled to the important museums in the state. It was fitting that Lew Dietz's tribute to Kosti, handsomely mounted, provided the accompanying text.

We slouch in deep chairs friendly to backsides. My tea is laced with rum. I tell Lew about this book on the Maine coast. He admits to a commitment for such a book himself, a commitment of long standing.

"Where does one begin?" he wants to know. "There's too much. Maine's too rich in lore and legend, in people. A dedicated writer could settle down in any one of a hundred towns along this coast. If he wrote only about the worthwhile and interesting things he encountered in his surroundings, wrote about them every day, eight hours a day for the rest of his life, and lived to be a hundred and ten, he'd only have scratched the surface of that one town."

Lew should know. He's one of Maine's most thoroughly professional writers. *The Allagash,* in the Rivers of America series is the definitive contemporary work on Maine's famed wilderness river. His outdoor stories and articles are published everywhere, often

reprinted and quoted. He is much sought after as a speaker on the Maine nature scene. He has hiked, climbed, canoed and explored most of the rugged face of Maine. Lew is lean, amiable, grizzled. A pensive, unhurried man, reliable under pressure.

"I first saw Maine in a two-week fog mull. I wandered into the state in 1930, a footloose kid. I was looking for something, I suppose; roots maybe, a place that went with my old clothes, a place that wasn't going to change every time my back was turned. Anyway, fog and all, I recognized home. As with hats or love, home is a matter of recognition. I responded to the low-key color of Maine, its textures; I warmed to its people. First it was the sea that took hold of me, then the woods. I expect at the time I was going through what is called today an identity crisis. Once in Maine, I suddenly knew who I was and where I belonged. Maine has been my home for forty years. I've never had the itch to look for another."

For many years, Peggy Bacon was a celebrated figure in New York art circles, famed for her sharp wit and her satirical pen-and-ink and brush sketches. Her two collections of pictures and verse, *Animosities* and *Cat-calls,* received high praise from the late Edmund Wilson.

Peggy lives year round in a trim white clapboard cottage at Cape Porpoise, still actively engaged in painting. I ask her if she finds the winters in Maine lonely.

"I'm not a person who ever gets lonely, but I have no close pals up here."

"What about the summertime?"

"Then I have as much social life as I need, which isn't very much."

"Do you miss New York?"

"I miss the museums and the galleries very much. And the few friends I have left. But I'm at an age now when so many of my friends have died that there really isn't so much of a pull to New York as there used to be."

I remind Peggy of a painting her ex-husband, Alexander Brook, had done, a painting of Peggy holding a cat. I try to remember the cat's name.

"Metaphysics," Peggy says smiling. "The title of the painting was *Peggy Bacon with Metaphysics.*"

We speak of artists of her generation — Marin, Burchfield, the Zorachs. She shows me an exquisite small sculpture by Zorach. "A lovely thing. He told me that it's very difficult to carve a very hard stone as small as that, and he did only four of them. He gave one to Marguerite, his wife; one to his daughter, Dahlov; one to Jacob Epstein; and this one to me. I'm proud of it and enjoy it. It has sentimental as well as artistic value. There's something quite wonderful about the color and texture of the stone."

I ask Peggy what it was like being an artist in New York during the Depression.

"Curiously enough, it was rather a good time for artists. The rich felt so poor that they couldn't go to Europe to buy old masters; so they more or less turned to the American artists. They could buy them for so much less and still be patrons of the arts."

What about the arts in this part of Maine?

"We get many painters and sculptors, especially in the summer. There's the Ogunquit Museum, open three months of the year, a beautiful building. Henry Strater built it in memory of his parents, I believe. The approach to it is in itself lovely. You go up a long pebble walkway, and as you go through the building you see the ocean on the other side. There's a sculpture garden outside. It's a small museum in the sense that it has no old masters. It's mostly contemporary."

What kind of painting is Peggy Bacon doing today?

"I'm very interested in mixed media ink and watercolor. I paint some in oils. I haven't done any etchings or lithographs for a number of years. I got very interested in color and now I'm having a show, a retrospective, at Nasson College in Springvale." She smiles. "I'm seventy-six. One goes on and on, doesn't one?"

The road to the Jamie Wyeths climbs the hill past the Odoms' general store and The Trailing Yew, turns into a crooked path marked with granite outcroppings and winds downhill toward the sea across one of Mr. Charles Francis Jenney's "waving moors." The weathered house is cedar shingled and white-trimmed. Built by Rockwell Kent, it stands alone, four-square to the sea. The almost desolate setting smacks of the Cornish coast and Land's End, stiff autumn sedge darkly rustling and the sea air damp against my cheek.

Jamie greets me in the entry. Still bemused by the Brontëan spell of the windswept moor, I see him as Heathcliff, but only for a moment. This cheerful young man smiles warmly, his grip is firm. The last vestige of Victorian gloom vanishes in the presence, moments later, of his wife, Phyllis, who is fresh-looking and lovely.

We settle down in the living room. Huge windows over a streaked stone promontory command an unbroken and seemingly limitless view of the sea. A powerful surf smashes unseen against the rocks below, a deep rumbling counterpoint to silence, oddly comforting. We talk of small matters at first, mostly local, getting to know each other. I ask Jamie if he uses Kent's old studio, over on Horn Hill.

"No, I don't own that. I've been coming out here all my childhood and the only place on the island I ever wanted to live was right here."

"Did you ever meet Kent?"

"Not really, but I wrote to him a couple of times before he died. I'd bought this large painting that he'd done out here. They're very difficult to find, you know. The Monhegan ones. Somehow a dealer located one for me and I bought it. I wrote Kent a letter saying I'd bought the house and also the painting. He wrote back marvelous letters describing how he built the house and what not. Amazing letters, full of detail . . ."

We discuss for a while Kent's persecution because of his political views. "I don't understand it," Jamie says with warmth. "I don't see why a man's work should suffer because of his politics. It's a shame the way they put Kent down. The perfect example was a museum right here in Maine. At one point, they were going to build an enormous wing for Kent. He was going to give all those paintings to the city. Then all of a sudden the McCarthy

hearings started and the board said, Nix, forget it. It was ridiculous. My grandfather, my mother's father, was one of the few people on the board who defended him. He stood up and said, 'You're making a terrible mistake. This man's politics had nothing to do with his paintings. These are great paintings and someday they'll really be fantastic. They're the best paintings ever done on these Maine islands.' It was no use.

"A friend of ours, a writer, was in Leningrad a couple of years ago. He spent a week in the Hermitage, which he says, without doubt, is the greatest museum in the world. The last day he was there, he walked into this room with Rockwell Kent's name over the door and here were forty paintings of Monhegan. In Leningrad!"

We talk of the tragic fire that destroyed Kent's studio and home in upstate New York a few years ago. "At that time," Jamie says, "a Rockwell Kent show was being mounted in the Walker Art Gallery at Bowdoin College and a lot of his paintings were saved."

I ask Jamie if his work is influenced by his father's style. Many people seem to think so. "Not consciously," he says. "And I never really was taught by my father. Funny thing. Whenever I'd finish a painting I'd call him and he'd come in and make general statements about the painting. He wouldn't say, 'That ear is badly drawn.' He'd say something about watching the form. He always says he's a terrible teacher. Well, God, that's the best way to teach. I mean, how can you conceivably tell someone that they're using the wrong color? There's no way in the world you can say that. Everyone has his own particular strange way of seeing things."

"I was thinking of the constancy of style," I say, "both in your father's and in your paintings. A changelessness. And I wonder if this is deliberate. Picasso, for example, is completely unpredictable in what he will do next." I go on to point out Picasso's boundless energy, the untiring artistic curiosity that drives him time and again to daring experiments and radical techniques.

"I don't know that much about Picasso as a person," Jamie explains. "But I think he's an innovator—one of those people who's constantly experimenting with new things and tires quickly of them. There are many different approaches to painting and experimentation is certainly one. I think Picasso is phenomenal, of course, and his greatness, the *real* greatness, of Picasso, is the man himself. He must just be extraordinary." He is thoughtful for a few long moments. "If you mean, will I change?—I'm sure—I *hope* I'll change. But the problem with a representational painter is, there's not a lot of tangible, *visual* change. I mean, I'm experimenting all the time when I'm painting, but it's not a radical change of style. Change just isn't readily apparent in a representational painter's style, but it's going on all the time."

I ask Jamie if living on an island limits him in any way. "Not at all. A lot of people suggest that eventually I'm going to run out of subjects to paint. I could stay right on this point and spend the rest of my life painting. All of my childhood I wanted to live aboard a boat— always an exciting idea. But, you know, when you're on a boat three weeks, it gets pretty crampy. This island is perfect for me. This house is like a boat but you also have the land."

68

"And you don't have to scrape the hull of an island."

"Right. To me, an island is a microcosm of a continent. I look at things growing around here as if they weren't carried, but simply formed here from whatever grew."

"Are you doing any seascapes?"

"I've never painted the surf or the sea. A lot of people think: Well, he's moved to an island and it's going to be me-and-seascapes. Well, the sea's *in* the things I've painted, but they're not seascapes."

"What do you think about abstract painting?"

"Terribly exciting. And I think a good representational painting can be exciting in its abstract forms. Do you know, if you could see a painting of mine in the beginning, it's one of the most abstract things imaginable. Then you start bringing it down. But it starts out wild."

I asked Jamie if he ever took one of his finished representational paintings and worked it down piece by piece to an abstraction. Maybe to a dozen abstractions.

"I've often abstracted things I've painted. You look at the painting and at the actual thing painted and they're quite different. Whether or not that's a pure abstraction, I don't know. A painter friend of mine does just that. He'll take a lamp or something and blow it up on the wall and fragment it in paint. My particular interest doesn't lie in that."

What about early training?

"My only formal training was a year with my aunt, Carolyn Wyeth, just drawing cubes and shapes. A horribly dull year, but valuable because it reinforced a certain lack of form. Then I studied anatomy for a year. Those were the only two formal periods of study I had."

"Have you worked in New York much?"

"Oh, yes. The last time, a couple of winters ago, after staying through late fall on Monhegan. I was working hard and at the time it was terribly exciting. It was such a change from Monhegan, you see. I got to know a lot of the painters. There's this restaurant where a lot of the painters hang out. All these guys come in, they sit up until four in the morning talking about what they're doing. I can think of nothing more enervating. I'm so goddam tired the next morning I can't work. And all that talk takes a lot of the excitement away from what you're working on. You talk it away. Not that the others'll know what you're doing. But I think you're taking away a certain mystery . . . I don't just know what it is—"

"You're spoiling the freshness of it in your own mind."

"Exactly."

"When a writer tells me the plot of a story he wants to write, I begin to doubt his ever writing it. Same with a painter who explains to me what his painting is supposed to mean and why he painted it. Hell! Once he shows it, it will tell its own story and it will be a different story to different people."

Jamie agrees. "When you've finished a painting, that's it. You're finished with it."

Our conversation shifts to the commercial galleries in Manhattan. I tell Jamie about the years before the war when I was a student at the Art Students League. A dozen or so galleries were clustered in the vicinity of Madison Avenue and Fifty-seventh Street. The names slip through my mind like faded calling cards. Action was slow. Galleries looked like half-abandoned funeral parlors in those Depression days, except for the Corots and Turners, Manets, Monets, Cezannes, Braques, Picassos and Rouaults that graced the walls. You could touch them. No one seemed to mind. They were pleased to see someone in their gallery — even a student just looking.

"My God," Jamie says. "Do you know how many galleries there are in New York today? Over two thousand! I'm snooping around them all the time, seeing what's going on. Most of the stuff, well — it just reinforces my idea of what I want to do."

The image of Wyeth men is well recognized. What about Wyeth women? What are they like?

"The amazing thing about my mother," Jamie says, "is that she married my father when she was seventeen. She says she knew nothing about painting then and sort of really grew up into it. The family name was James. Her father actually did paint. He was the editor of a newspaper in New York and all of a sudden he decided, the hell with this, and just picked up and moved to Maine. Cushing. Their farm is up from my father's. He was about twenty-three then and they sort of grew up together. She's devoted her whole life to him and his work, which is really extraordinary. And of course, my grandmother's still living, N. C. Wyeth's wife. She's remarkable. She's eighty-five and still quite active. She still has the house over in Port Clyde. Then there's my aunt, Carolyn Wyeth —"

And there's Phyllis, quiet and attentive through much of our conversation. She's a Mills from Long Island. I recall watching her father, Sonny Mills, play polo with the crack Meadowbrook Club four back in the thirties. She's pleased I remember him. Phyllis doesn't paint but has more than a passing interest in the art world. She smiles. "How can I not be interested?"

Visitors arrive, a neighbor and a gaggle of children. Phyllis excuses herself. I ask Jamie why neither he nor his father has ever traveled abroad.

"I'd probably find it difficult to work in a place I don't know. I get itchy when I travel. Even when I'm doing portraits, it's usually of people I've known. It's important to me to know where they've lived and what they've done all their lives. All that goes into the portrait. You take the people who come here in the summer, and stay maybe three or four days or even a week and they leave and they tell their friends they've seen Monhegan Island. They see *nothing!* They haven't scratched the surface. All they do is see something and eyeball it and move on."

I tell Jamie that by travel I really mean expatriating oneself. As American painters did a generation or two ago. Says Jamie: "But why? Why should I work anywhere else? I mean, even if I were born in New York City and lived on Third Avenue in the heart of things, I'd feel the same way. Not that it's so spectacular here, or so beautiful. It's just that it's a place I've known almost all my life. And I can dig deeper and deeper. There are people here I can paint because I know what affects them and what goes on organically with them. Maybe as I mature I might want to travel, but at this point to pick up and move to a place for five years — ? I see no need for it."

He's lucky, I tell him, knowing so early in life what he wants of it.

"I never doubted it," Jamie says. "I pretty much cut myself off when I left school, mainly because I wanted to paint. It's the only thing that really excited me. I tried a lot of things, testing this or that to see where my interest went and quite frankly and quite simply, painting was the only thing that turned me on. The only thing in which I was totally interested and wanted to do. It's really that simple."

I didn't believe it. Zero Mostel? Here on Monhegan? Impossible! Monhegan's an island surrounded by water. Zero Mostel's an island surrounded by people. But who else could get two islands together, one on top of the other? There was his house on a slope of land, a long stone's throw from the Wyeths. Zero's studio (he comes to the island to paint and relax) is perched alongside Herb Kallem's. Herb and Zero also have studios in mid-Manhattan. This one on Monhegan is a sightly place, cedar shingled, overlooking the harbor and the island called Manana with no enya over the *n*.

Zero first came to Monhegan in the thirties, with New York painters like Joseph Kaplan and Joe DeMartini, looking for an isolated, inexpensive summer place to work. Monhegan filled the bill. It was hard to get to, unspoiled, and living was cheap. In those Depression summers, Zero found time to adapt a Molière play. His studio was out of doors: a big flat rock. It was here, during one of those Monhegan summers, that his friend Clifford Odets wrote his play *Country Girl.*

Then with fame it became a sanctuary of sorts for Zero. "Listen," he says. "To sit down and eat dinner and the phone doesn't ring, is an accomplishment hard to come by these days."

He is ebullient, Falstaffian, Chaucerian. Also Tevyan. A walking fun palace with a fox in the bush. His booming laughter can shatter thick plate glass. He was a damned good painter long before he became a damned good actor. He works hard and loves to work hard at both trades.

The Mostels have no phone on Monhegan. A long-distance call for Zero came to the Odoms' general store one day. Doug Odom answered. It was Hollywood calling. Very urgent, the party said. "I'll take the message and give it to him," said Doug. The party was insistent. He was a Hollywood producer, he announced. It was imperative that he speak with Zero Mostel in person and at once. "In that case," Odom said, "he's out with the herring fleet and won't be back for several days." And hung up.

I ask Zero what kind of reception the islanders give a resident Broadway star. He shrugs "They leave you alone. Like they do anyone else. The marvelous thing about these people is their anarchism. They don't interfere. But if you're looking for help, it's always there when you need it."

He reminisces about the island people. Like Joe Pease, who comes over from Thomaston. Master carpenter, craftsman, fisherman, Joe built Zero's house. Zero chuckles and the floor trembles. "Joe has that pure dry Yankee wit. He'll get off the mail boat and when she's leaving for the mainland stand there on the boat landing and mutter, 'Marooned again.'"

Dwight Stanley's one of Zero's favorite island people. Dwight was king of the lobstermen in his heyday. Stories and articles have been written about his salty exploits in a dozen national magazines over the years. Dwight holds court these days in his upstairs fish loft. He calls it his "Fix-it shop." Dwight is a formidable poker player, but for all his years in boats, he can't swim a stroke.

Zero also remembers the time he bought a cast-iron piano from June Day for his wife Kathryn. The problem was to get it from June's cottage on the beach up to the Mostels. The volunteer piano bearers, besides Zero and Kallem, included Wyeth, DeMartini and a few other artists. "A million dollars worth of talent," Zero moans, "schlepping one lousy cast-iron piano and risking mass hernia."

He admits to occasional lapses of propriety that sometimes startle the unwary observer but never fail to relieve the monotony. One time, approaching the island, he prevailed on Captain Fields to lash him to the mast. With his eyes rolled back and his tangled beard waving in the wind, he could not have failed (except for his reassuring bulk) to remind the astonished crowd of a crazed though oddly rabbinical Ancient Mariner.

And in his more profound and theatrical moments, he has been known to stand on the crowded boat landing as the *Laura B.* comes alongside with yet another boatload of tourists, waving it off and shouting, "Plague! Plague! Cholera! Go back!"

Plague shmague. Zero always goes back to Monhegan himself. He always will. "You come here year after year and nothing's changed. You know something? If Monhegan was a Greek island, Onassis would own it."

People lucky enough to know E. B. White call him "Andy." Some of them probably wonder where the nickname comes from. Well. Elwyn Brooks White went to Cornell. The first president of Cornell was Andrew Dickson White (1832–1918). After that, anyone who went to Cornell whose name was White was automatically called "Andy."

White lives year round in Maine with his wife Katharine. She was co-editor of their 1941 book, *A Subtreasury of American Humor*. White is a thoughtful farmer and public defender of brown eggs. He began his writing career by submitting pieces to *The New Yorker* and eventually became one of its most revered contributing editors. He has published three books for children, *Stuart Little*, *Charlotte's Web* and, most recently, *The Trumpet of the Swan*. Some of them are classics.

Long before the phrase "population explosion" became a household caveat White wrote, with James Thurber, a very funny book called *Is Sex Necessary?* (1929). For this Penn freshman at that time it was a dazzling revelation of how to get on with the opposite sex without really worrying. Now the population explosion may be threatening the Maine way

of life. It seemed a good idea to ask "Andy" White to comment on it, perhaps calling it *Is Maine Necessary?*

"Hereabouts," White reports, "the population has not exploded: in our town more deaths have been reported lately than births. And this part of Maine is not a great deal more populous, generally speaking, than it was forty years ago, when I bought our home. There is, however, a greater tidal movement, a greater flow in and out during the summertime because of the nomadic quality of American life these days. Young people limit their families; instead of building a house, many of them buy a second-hand trailer and set it up in someone's back yard or at the edge of a woodlot, for instant living. Visitors arrive in campers trailing an outboard, or they arrive in a station wagon with a canoe balanced on top and a motorbike strapped to the tailgate. They are restless, searching, always on the move. But summer visitors are nothing new around here. The house I live in was accepting boarders seventy-five years ago, when Hattie Joyce lived here. Six dollars a week was the tariff, and that included everything—meals, bed and a view of the water. People arrived by steamboat. They brought no equipment but instead brought a quiet mind, which is sometimes a happier arrangement.

"Is Maine necessary? All locales are necessary. I liked it better here when there was passenger service on the railroad—the space shuttle will be a sorry substitute for that. Maine occupies a special place in the hearts of many. I think it will survive."

JOURNAL NOTE: Maine has another celebrated "Andy," named Wyeth. Like White, he's shy of publicity and would be perfectly content to be known only as Jamie Wyeth's father. I met "Andy" Wyeth and his wife Betsy at a dinner reception given for him by Governor and Mrs. Kenneth Curtis at Blaine House.

Wyeth cuts a smart figure in evening clothes. He wore what must be the only pair of imported patent leather dancing pumps in the state of Maine. I say *imported*. I cannot believe there's a Maine storekeeper alive with the courage to stock dancing pumps along with his hunting boots and buffalo plaids. These had to come from as far away as Boston.

Wyeth appeared worried. He confided to me the publication of a definitive work on his art was imminent. His publisher had told Wyeth the limited autographed edition would be offered at $2,500 a copy. Wyeth was astonished. Who'd ever pay a price like that?

He had nothing to worry about. The edition was a sellout.

Young and old, they beat a path to his door. If he's relaxing on his island hideaway off Deer Isle, they make it there by boat or canoe.

He's the closest thing in Maine to a Renaissance Man. Architect, author, scientist, philosopher—the labels of intellectual accomplishment go on and on. And living on Bear Island summers since 1905, Buckminster Fuller's a damned good sailor. What attracts the believers, however, is his firm faith in the future of our shaky civilization. Science and technology, he predicts, will bring all the people of the world together in a kind of healthy interdependence. Attacking another nation will become as unthinkable as one part of a town attacking the other end of the same town.

He admires and is very much encouraged by the controversial younger generation whose members refuse to lie and instead tell the truth as they see it. He finds this "extraordinary, beautiful and logical."

During the bitter controversy over oil refineries along Maine's seacoast, Fuller wrote a lengthy poem/telegram to Senator Ed Muskie, which the *New York Times* reprinted in March of 1971. One stanza in mid-poem reveals eloquently the depth of Fuller's feelings:

> *It is economic ignorance of the lowest order*
> *To persist in further surfacing and expenditure*
> *Of the earth's fossil fuels—*
> *It is even more ignorant and irresponsible*
> *To surface and transport oils*
> *Of Arabia, Venezuela, Africa and East Indies*
> *To refineries and storages on the coast of Maine*
> *This putting into ecological jeopardy*
> *One of the world's*
> *As yet most humanly cherished*
> *Multi-islanded, sea coast wildernesses.*
> *In view of Fundy's tidal energy wealth*
> *Such blindness is more preposterous*
> *Than "carrying coals to Newcastle."*
> *It is accelerated human suicide.*

Harness the power of Passamaquoddy's semi-completed tidal generation system, Fuller insists. It was abandoned for politically selfish reasons through the lobbying interests of several major Maine industries that themselves were polluting the rivers and destroying Maine's once abundant fisheries.

> *I pray you will make your stand*
> *Swiftly and unambiguously clear*
> *As being against any further incursions*
> *Of petroleum into Maine*
> *Or of pipelines in Alaska.*

Poet, too. And humanitarian.

84

MAN AND THE SEA

Sea is an ageless word worn smooth with time. Its sound slips easily from the lips, more sweetly than ocean; as autumn seems a sweeter word than fall. But nothing else about the sea comes easily. She's a touchy neighbor, an ancient friend and enemy and a good provider, sustaining, engulfing, tempting and taunting man since time began.

Man has seen miracles in that time and created wonders, but nothing yet to match the living sea. The moon is a dead place; the space ship as doomed as a Roman chariot. The convoluted ribbon of surf that fringes the Maine coast reveals nothing of the thirty-three million square miles of sea. Beneath the Atlantic's surface are six-mile-deep gorges like the Puerto Rico Trench. Above it are islands like Bermuda and the Azores; mountain peaks rooted more than twelve thousand feet below sea level. Her ebb and flow wash away the grandest dreams of man like sand castles. Her waves are the rhythm of all living things, bearing life and sucking it away.

The sea is the heaven and hell we came from and where one day we must return.

Consider the lobster.

Socially hostile. Cosmetically forbidding. But boiled, baked or stuffed and served up with melted lemon butter and a cold Chablis—a toothsome trip to paradise. Sing your praises of the abalone of California, or the prawn of Louisiana. Neither comes within a claw's clutch of *Homarus americanus*. Even the rare stone crab of Florida, enshrined in its gaudy orange and black porcelain, runs a soggy second to Maine's succulent lobster.

Lobstering in Maine averages out to about twenty million pounds a year, the largest catch along the Atlantic coast. There's another catch: a lobster dinner may run anywhere from six to twelve dollars. Yet the lobsterman who risks his life to bring the delicacy to your table averages about a buck and a half a pound for his labors. At fifty pounds a haul, three times a week, he grosses less than two hundred dollars. There's a Catch 22, of course. Too many good hauls drive the market price down.

Out of his weekly gross he must pay for his boat, maintenance and repairs to the hull and engine, to his gear and tackle, his buoys and traps. He needs bait (redfish, alewives or herring cuttings) and a few cold beers to warm him. If anything's left, it goes to feed and clothe his family and pay the mortgage or rent.

Sometimes he feels the whole world's against him. The weather in one blow can wipe out half his traps, smash his hull, drown his engine, wreck his gear. Or it can simply keep him from getting outside to earn his living.

The law gives him a hard time, setting rules and regulations on what he can catch and where. Lately, in a flood of scare statistics on the mercury level in test samples of New England lobsters, the public health officials are also giving him a hard time.

Little wonder a smile on a lobsterman's face is as rare as a suntan in midwinter Maine. Here are excerpts from a lobster report culled at random from the *National Fisherman* of June 1971: A fire aboard Robert Smith's boat out of Jonesport, as she prepared to go shrimping at about 4 A.M., caused damage estimated at $2,000. Fishermen around Portland and Boothbay report heavy wharf damage from ice floes and high winds. From the Vinalhaven-to-New Harbor reporter: Price for one-and-a-quarter-pound lobsters dropped from $1.30 to $1.20 a pound.

Why be a lobsterman? The answer is simple. His father was a lobsterman. And his grandfather. Lobstermen are a rugged proud breed, apart from the world of other fishermen. Everything about them reflects their unique life style, their roots in the pioneer American heritage.

The first look at the lobsterman's world is a memorable one. Traps in sunlight and shadow are stacked in a geometric maze. Brightly painted buoys gleam like racing silks, hung, strung, drying from rafters in the fish shanties. The lobster boats—Jonesporters, Friendships or Gamage-built wave-busters from South Bristol—and even homemade hulls, ride the harbor's calm with a plain, sturdy grace, rough and in their odd way lovely, like the men who work them.

Men of the sea traditionally name their work boats for their women—the wives, mothers, daughters and sweethearts who wait and pray. The Greek honor *Areti* and *Katerina* and *Anthoula;* the French, *La Pauline, La Roberte* and even *La Joconde,* the Mona Lisa. The Spaniards' sardine boats in the Mediterranean pay homage to *Eulalia, Rosita* and *Brigida.* Out of Maine harbors sail *Betsy* and *Sally* and *Marcia Ann.* I wonder sometimes which is the true love—the lady or the boat. And I never heard of a fisherman's boat named for two, like *Connie & Linda.* It could only come to a bad end.

Take the lobsterman himself. Watch him work. Watch his eyes. Squinted from glare and cold, a spray of weather wrinkles in the tight skin over the corners. The cheeks drawn taut, wind tanned and briny. His open collar reveals paleness of skin below. If he happens to remove his work gloves, take a look at his hands. Big red knuckles. Old scars. A raw gash, sometimes festering. Winch, manila line, steel cable, knife, claw—these are his livelihood and his enemies. They tear through glove cloth like shark teeth. Setting traps or

hauling them, grabbing for markers, bending line or cable to a winch, handling the reluctant lobster, these are constant risks. I hold in high esteem any craftsman or carpenter over sixty who has all his fingers. The same goes for the lobsterman, only more so. His workshop is a rolling cockleshell at the mercy of the sea. Once outside, he has no way out of the weather unless he heads back. And loses a day's pay. So he fights the weather and stays with his traps. No lobsterman wants to come home empty-handed. It's a hurt to his pride. More so than to his pocketbook.

"I'd go out tomorrow," one retired old-timer says. "If'n my kids'll let me." He's over ninety now. He passes the time knitting nylon nets, called "heads," for lobster traps. A trap has two side heads attached to both ends of the pots, designed so the lobster can enter. The central or "bedroom" head inside holds the bait and prevents the lobster's escape.

The old-timer gets $1.50 a day and working steadily can knit fifteen heads. His hands are tough and gnarled. Thick callous grows where nylon rubs. It's not the money, he explains. It's having a hand in something to do with lobstering.

It's easy to understand. It's all they know. It's all they ever wanted to do. Father to son. But not alone for pleasure. "Who goes to sea for pleasure, would go to Hell for a pastime." Ask any lobsterman.

It's a strange feeling, walking around an old Maine boatyard. The ghosts are there. No need to see them. You feel and sometimes hear them. In the ravaged hulls of dry rot. Heaved ways. Shavings gray with age. Men still work in the huge shed. Power saws hum. Or screech. Sanders sing. Or scream. It's a wrong tune for ghosts. The wrong dress. Can you picture an old ghost in fiber glass?

What a sight it must have been, readying a wooden-hulled schooner for launching! Steaming and bending the oak frames. Adzing each timber. Pine planking her decks. Shaping and stepping her spruce masts. Caulking, painting, varnishing. Finally knocking loose the chocks and freeing her for sea.

A few years ago, Maine's Commission on the Arts and the Humanities gave Harvey Gamage a sculpture award "for his contribution to the State's cultural life." Gamage is one of a handful of boat builders left in Maine who are traditionalists in their craft. He's past seventy. He's given up hope of finding young men to continue the art of building wooden boats. Neither the pay nor the demand for such boats would warrant it.

The first Gamages to build boats were Harvey's two great-uncles. In 1854 they began work on the *Jenny Lind,* a ten-ton schooner, in the same South Bristol yard where Harvey more than a hundred years later launched the wooden-hulled *Bill of Rights.* A century ago, this launching would have scarcely drawn notice. The Maine coast was alive then with ship launchings and christenings.

But they came in droves this late March day in '71 to witness the rare event. Cars jammed the roads to South Bristol in all directions. A chartered bus drove all the way from Providence, Rhode Island. Out-of-state plates were seen everywhere.

Gamage built her in the true old-fashioned way. A topsail schooner, 125 feet overall, designed for the business pleasure of windjammer cruising. Oak-framed, with cedar sides, oak and fir planking and hard pine decks, *Bill of Rights* is a replica of a fast, mid-nineteenth-century gaff-rigged schooner that ran contraband along the Atlantic coast. A living ghost.

During the war, the Gamage yard built PT and YP boats for the Navy. Since 1944, the yard has completed more than 100 fishing vessels. The ninety-five-foot dragger *Albatross* received national recognition when the Smithsonian Institution designed and built a model of it for its marine collection.

A handful of wooden boat builders are still around. Perhaps now and then they take on a fiber glass job. Or a steel hull. Perhaps not. It doesn't matter. These ghosts of wooden boats are edgy. Ferro-cement hulls are no longer a fad. They're coming on strong.

Ever see a ghost in cement?

JOURNAL NOTE: Names of Maine places can be as whimsical as its people. Denmark and Sweden, Poland and China. Moscow and Naples, Sorrento and Verona. And Liberty, Unity, Hope and Freedom. Misery Gore, twenty-five miles long and less than a half mile wide, is in no township at all, having been the difference remaining after early township boundaries were corrected.

Within a few miles of my own village are Dunkertown, Promised Land, Suckerville, College Swamp, Jugtown and the Underwitted Road, this last getting its name because the road's width is narrower than the law allows.

And in Somerset County there's Desolation Pond and Tumbledown Mountain and Enchanted Stream. I've been there and they are.

Dennis Eaton at seventy-seven is relaxed and gentle, his frame well knit and hardy and the sea is in his eyes. When he was a boy his grandfather gave him two lobster traps and told him they were his to keep and what he harvested in them he could sell or eat. Dennis has been at it ever since, fishing out of Stonington. For a time in 1917 he worked in the Bath shipyard on the old coal-burning destroyers, and in a Massachusetts machinery shop. In Stonington he worked the air drills in the John L. Goss quarry. But lobstering was closest to his heart.

At his peak he was working 150 traps, ". . . alone by myself, but always in sight of Johnny Billings," just so they'd not get lost. These days he's back to the original two, ". . . just to keep a hand in, is all."

For a time he took himself and wife to Isle au Haut out in the harbor. He kept a flock of sheep on a nearby island he once owned, a fog-hung sweep of thick salt meadow. A rowdy flock it was and Dennis had to keep the ram on a separate island to maintain a sheepish peace. After his father died, he came back to the mainland to live out his years in his father's clapboard cottage, a trim red and yellow two-story affair facing the harbor.

He cultivates an ancient bed of wild lupine. Neglected, it had surrendered to the weeds over the years. Now tended by his skilled hands, it flourishes.

George is taking pictures. The harbor is gray mist. Dennis sits on the railing outside in the chill Maine morning in his heavy boots and thick woolen socks.

I ask him about something I had heard — that lobsters die from a broken claw. Dennis nods. "In hot weather maybe, or tangling with another lobster. The claw breaks off, sure. But nature's given the lobster a way to 'shoot it off,' you might say. That way, the end heals or another grows in its place."

"And if the lobster doesn't 'shoot it off'?"

"He bleeds, then, and dies."

I ask Dennis all sorts of questions about lobstering and the sea. He knows the answers and he doesn't talk down to me and I'm grateful for that.

George finishes. Mrs. Eaton reminds Dennis he has an appointment with his doctor for a checkup. Dennis sighs and his smile is bleak. Another day I must spend more time with him. We walk to his car with Mrs. Eaton. He turns to me.

"I always worked hard," he says in his slow, even Maine way. "Since I was a small boy. For my father and my grandfather before him. I did what they told me to do. Just followed in their footsteps and it was never the wrong thing and I never got hurt. All my life I have never known nothing but hard work and had I to do it over again, I wouldn't have no other way."

That was in May. The chill of Maine's worst winter in years was not yet out of my bones. We returned to Stonington early in August. The sun shone hard. The harbor sparkled. The green islands looked like soft velvet seals.

Mrs. Eaton met us at the door. Seeing us, her eyes filled. We knew at once the news was bad. Dennis had died at June's end, not too long after our visit.

We sat in the small parlor surrounded by a bereaved world of family portraits and bric-a-brac. It was his heart, she told us, looking brave. They had been told by the doctor to expect it. They never knew just when.

George had brought along a large print he had promised the Eatons. It was a portrait of Dennis on the railing, looking rugged and handsome. George handed it to her. It was too much for Mrs. Eaton. This time she wept. It was the last picture ever taken of Dennis, she told us. She would treasure it.

Outside, the lupine was in full bloom, its delicate, blue-fingered leaves arched against the blue of sky and sea. I remembered something I had read about lupine. Mediterranean people find the seeds a delicacy, but the plants are poisonous to cattle.

I wondered if Dennis had known that. He knew so much. If he did know, I don't suppose he really would have cared. Bringing the lupine to life was something useful to do, like hard work, until his time came.

A man working the sea has no friend more steadfast than a lighthouse. Day or night it gives him his bearings, constant warning of danger, reassuring comfort to his chilled bones. He depends on it as he does his compass and engine or sail.

The earliest lighthouses were simple structures topped by a beacon fire of wood or oil to guide Mediterranean fishermen and sailors seven hundred years before Christ. A lighthouse today consists of a dwelling place for the keeper (and his family if he has one), and the beacon tower itself. They are usually situated on coastline promontories, sunken rocks or shoals, or at harbor entrances and estuaries. Where the construction of buildings is impractical, lightships and light buoys are often used.

Modern lights are powered electrically, electronically, or by the combustion of acetylene gas. Their duties are often augmented by loran and other radio navigation systems. The light is concentrated and projected by a series of revolving lenses of decreasing thickness, called the dioptric or Fresnel lens. Alternated with straight refracting lenses on a revolving frame with an incandescent lamp at its center, the Fresnel lens produces a flash for each lens at each revolution of the frame.

Maine's oldest beacons were tended by a rugged breed of lighthouse keepers affectionately called "wickies." Today, United States Coast Guard personnel man the twenty-six lights from Isles of Shoals off York Beach to the candy-striped West Quoddy Head lighthouse, built in 1807. Some are called "stag lights" and others, "family lights," depending on the marital status of the resident crew. The Coast Guard also keeps a sharp eye on a number of unmanned lights still serving as aids to Maine coast navigators. A dozen or so have been abandoned or sold.

Gary Merrill, the actor, recently bought a lighthouse tower at Cape Elizabeth and plans to live in it as soon as alterations are completed. "I spent much of my childhood summers around here," Gary explains. "When I'm away I miss it very much. I like the smell of the ocean. I like hearing the sound of the waves and the silence."

His first name's James, but his friends call him Pebble. He builds fine Maine boats in a handsome Norse structure that's part boatyard, part dwelling. But no one else in the world builds his boats where Pebble does—on a mountain top with a sweeping view of Penobscot Bay in the distance.

"Why on a mountain top, Pebble?"

"Why not? Once she's ready, it's downhill all the way."

Pebble's from Connecticut. I ask him why he chose Maine. "I like the Maine idea," he says, and grins. "My idea of Maine is well-built boats."

He's been sailing boats since he was a school kid. When he came to Maine he thought a lot about getting into the boat business, and one day everything sort of fell into place and he began to build a boat.

"When you decide to build a boat in Maine, of course, the first one has to be a Friendship sloop. That's the logical place to start. After one Friendship sloop came another

Friendship sloop; and from a Friendship sloop came a conventional-type power boat. It's sort of gone along from there. I've tried to set it up so that I wouldn't have to do too many of one kind. Life is so short you have to crowd in as much variety as you possibly can. I like different projects. That's the reason I'm building airplanes now."

The delicate wood skeleton of a small plane under construction in a corner of the work shed looks too fragile to fly, as though a buffeting by the first cross wind would smash it like an eggshell.

"Are planes trickier to build?"

"Easier in construction, compared to boats. The beauty of it is, every little bit of wood there counts for something. It has real integrity, more so even than a boat. Boats, especially these little Friendships, are way overbuilt. You can take out a lot of wood and it will still float and carry you safely. With an airplane you just can't spare any of that material."

"What kind of plane is this one going to be?"

"Strictly a Red Baron type."

"Your first one?"

"Yes. I hope it's not the last."

"Would you compare Maine flying with Maine sailing?"

"The Maine coast's a marvelous place for sailing. Wonderful cruising grounds and not too many other boats. A little pollution, perhaps, but not too bad. Same with a plane. We don't have too many in the air to run into. There's a little fog to contend with. A few mountains. That's about all."

"Won't it get worse?"

"I would like to think that Maine might stay small and simple. We once had a big boat man from Long Island come into Rockland to turn out boats and employ a lot of people. Which he did. But anything that survives in Maine more or less starts out quite small and grows from there. It's a mistake to come in here big. Everything that's come into Maine big right off has gone to hell in a matter of years. This fellow went to pot. Another man came into town a few years ago. His idea was to have every boat for sale in the United States put through a computer. A lot of folks believed in him. They said this is the greatest thing that's ever happened to Maine."

"What happened?"

"He lasted just one year. In my business I come across a lot of people who have done a little bit of everything. A little bit of this, a little bit of that. Maine doesn't seem to be the country for the promoter, thank goodness."

"You find any young people interested in boat building?"

"I have one young fellow who's worked for me since we came here. Several months ago, to my horror, he said he was going to leave me. For no good reason. It wasn't the pay or anything, he said, but he had got a chance to run a bulldozer. It was too bad, because in the course of four or five years, he had really got the knack of putting wood together. He did beautiful cabinet work and I hated to think of him running a bulldozer.

Well, he left and he was back in two weeks. Decided he liked boat building better after all. He found out that running big machinery wasn't that romantic."

"Why all this interest in the Friendship sloop? Is it that great a boat?"

"Actually, it's a very impractical boat. Hard to sail and there's very little room. But they are quite fast. I think it's their history that makes them popular. And the people who sail them seem to like each other. If you're along the Maine coast and in a Friendship sloop, somebody's liable to come up and say hello to you, where they wouldn't think of it if you were in a stock boat. It's like an old car club."

"Do you have a boat of your own?"

"An old lobster boat, yes, built back in '48. She's thirty-seven feet. I broke down and had the engine overhauled this year. Then I have a little eighteen-foot cutter and various small boats."

"You've sailed to Tahiti, haven't you?"

"In '51, yes. She was a Friendship, a big one, rigged as a ketch. One of the few ever rigged that way."

"Did you like Tahiti?"

"I didn't mind it. I stayed there ten months. I've nothing bad to say about Tahiti except you wouldn't want to live there. I stayed just about the right amount of time and I think if I was any older then, I wouldn't have been able to stay there six months. Tahiti was very beautiful then. I went back a couple of years ago and it's completely changed. It's just another tourist spot."

"Like Maine?"

Pebble smiles. "Not at all. Not at all like Maine."

A blaze in a boatshop on Portland's Commercial Street started the worst fire in its history. It very nearly destroyed the entire city. That was on Independence Day in 1866. Since then, Portland's waterfront has had its up and downs, riding the waves of world wars and depressions as staunchly as the ships that come and go through Casco Bay.

Can a waterfront truly change? The sea is there and men still profit on its harvest. Portland is a poorer port today than fifty years ago. Commercial Street is still the wholesale marketplace for the city and for much of the rest of the state. Old Yankee names like Twitchell Champlin are gone. So is Swift & Company. Hannaford and Milliken Tomlinson are removed to suburban industrial parks. A few store fronts look familiar; paper and twine dealers, a ships' chandlery, the old-time fruit wholesalers. I park the car along the rusting train tracks.

A big sign painted on a building tells me I'm in Boone Country but the street sign says Union Wharf. I stop by Leavitt & Parris, sailmakers. The original Parris started at fourteen and quit at eighty. He made canvas for the Union Army. The last of the Parris family died in 1969. Now Jim Greenleaf runs the place. I talk to Charley Hitton in the sail loft. He's got some canvas stretched out on the deck (floor) but takes time off to chat with me.

Charley's worked here for over twenty years. He tells me Leavitt & Parris still make custom sails. They also turn out awnings and chair covers and navy tops. "Anything," Charley says, "you can make out of a piece of canvas. But none of the big stuff. The fancy yachts. Not much call for it these days."

Sam Armstrong has been handling lobsters for twenty-five years at the New Meadows Lobster Pound on Portland Pier. I tell Sam that's the least likely name for a lobster company I ever heard. He grins and explains that his father ran the New Meadows Inn in West Bath for years and named the lobster company after the inn.

Sam stores his lobsters in tanks with salt water in constant circulation. The tanks are kept filled with fresh-caught Maine and Canadian lobsters throughout the year except during the bad weather months from January through March, at which time lobsters kept live in pounds along the coast are marketed.

The chain of demand is something like this: fisherman to dock buyer (like Sam), to trucker and airline, to wholesaler, to wholesaler's agent, to restaurant or retailer, to consumer—enough good reasons to explain the cost of a lobster dinner.

Fast air service has greatly expanded today's market. Shipments are made practically anywhere overnight, weather permitting. Summer prices are generally lower because lobsters are shedding their shells. Shedders spend a few weeks in hiding, usually starting around the first of July. They do not go in search of food because the lack of protection makes them vulnerable to attack. When they begin to crawl again they are starved and trap more readily. With the heavier catch prices are normally lower. The new shell lobster has a superior flavor but is not strong and cannot be shipped live long distances.

The state at one time tried to control the rearing of lobsters to provide a steady market, maximum yield and good quality. But the cannibal instinct of the lobster defeated the project. Lobsters will attack and eat each other while in the weak shedding period.

On Central Wharf at the Willard-Daggett Fish Company, Johnny Cogswell and his men have just finished smoking a batch of bloaters (small herring, really). The aroma is tantalizing. The bloaters hang in neat rows on the drying racks. They gleam like old gold. Men are filleting flounder in the next room. Their knives flash in the dull morning light. I cannot help think it must have been like this in every ancient fish house of the world.

I recall a conversation with the late Jack Willard in the office upstairs. A huge hibiscus plant languished near the window in the winter sun. Jack was a trim, laconic, silver-haired Yalie whose family has been dealing in fresh fish since the turn of the century. The Willard-Daggett trawler fishing fleet had been one of the best along the Maine coast. Recently they decided to give it up. I asked Jack why.

The waterfront was slipping, he told me. There was no freight business. Buildings were deteriorating. Wharves were drifting away. Pilings disappeared overnight in the slimy water.

Air freight is expensive. There had once been a New York boat back in the twenties and a fast freight every morning. But no more. Trawling paid off in ports like New Bedford where there were large-volume catches and a close market, but Portland was just too risky.

Jack leaned back and stared bleakly through the hibiscus at the cold gray harbor. "All a boat is," he said, "is a big hole in the water surrounded by wood and steel into which you dump money."

Outside, I walk back along Portland Wharf past torn asbestos shingles and bright orange shrimp nets and the sagging tin-sheeted shells of the old fish houses. Everything, it seems, needs roofing nails. Stacked lobster pots stuccoed with barnacles lean crookedly against oil drums stinking of fish waste.

On Commercial Street I draw a few deep breaths and stare down its broad expanse to the awesome shape of the Grand Trunk Railway's grain elevator #2, rearing skyward like a monolithic Tower of Babel. It's a structure you cannot forget. Grain elevator #1 was torn down thirty years ago. This one, with a capacity of eighty-four million pounds, hasn't been used since 1967. A tombstone to Portland's waterfront boom days. I head west for Merchants Wharf and a lobster fisherman named Lloyd Cushing.

Lloyd Cushing is a Portland native, twenty-nine years old, skipper of his own lobster boat, *Miss Juli.* She's a fifty-foot, steel-hulled, diesel-powered beauty rebuilt to his specific needs by Blount Marine in Rhode Island. I have never seen such a lobster boat. The below decks area is spacious and comfortably equipped. The powerful diesel sits amidships, easy to work over if need be.

Lloyd is modest about it, pleased with my praise. He's solidly built, apple-cheeked, a serious young man respected by his salty seagoing colleagues. He's married and has three children. He's been a fisherman for over ten years. His father and grandfather were lobstermen. He never thought to do anything else. "It's in a man's blood," he says.

He admits lobstering's a funny business. "It's unique. A man can go into it big or small." Lloyd decided on big. He chose diesel and he chose radar. He installed the first automatic trap hauler on the coast. It can work up to seven hundred traps and give the lobsterman ten times the freedom he had before. He uses conveyors and his catch is handled at the dock by lift trucks and pallets. He uses bigger traps because the automatic equipment calls for less muscle. Lloyd's brother, David, helps in the dockside workshop and at sea. The Cushings build their own traps, using mechanized labor-saving devices. The traps are machine-cut and power-stapled. A retired lobsterman, Charley Train, eighty-nine, makes the nylon heads for the traps. Redfish and cod heads make the best bait, Lloyd tells me.

In spite of the hardships and setbacks of the business, the next generation is coming right along. I'm impressed and I tell this to Lloyd Cushing. He thinks about it for a while.

"You're an old man before you have anything to say in a business. It's rare now that you can have a say in any business, young or old. I'm in a small business where I want to be and I have the say and I'm doing what I like best."

Lloyd's father, Stanley, drowned fourteen years ago when Lloyd was fifteen. A line

caught around his hand when he was fishing alone in his thirty-six-foot Jonesporter and he was dragged under. It was a Monday, Lloyd remembers.

JOURNAL NOTE: I'm convinced most of Portland's restaurants are fed on a moving belt from a central kitchen in the subcellars of City Hall. There can be no other explanation for the identical bills of fare, the monotony of choice, the lackluster appearance of the food, the dull institutional taste of just about everything.

Meats taste as though they died of freezer burn. Bread and rolls have the warmed-over crunch of yesterday. Roquefort dressing costs an extra dime or quarter. Potatoes are baked, french fried, or mashed, period. Fresh-caught haddock or halibut out of Maine's own waters may appear on the menu but not on your plate. "It must've been fresh before they froze it," the waitress insists.

This is seacoast Maine, once a proud place of fisherfolk and fine fresh seafood. The pride is gone. Today, if a whole live lobster could be frozen and sold, they'd freeze it.

One of the reasons outside people envy Maine people is their mistaken impression that we sit around all day stuffing our faces with fresh lobster because it's cheap and plentiful. The truth of it is, Maine people get to see less lobster on their table than anyone else. Most of the catch is shipped to Boston and New York. Right now, in March of 1972, the lobster business is the worst it's ever been. There's precious little to ship. Northeast storms have raised hell with the lobsterman's traps and gear. One fisherman who averages over two thousand pounds a week, year round, from his traps, took in a scant fifty pounds in four days last week.

Weather isn't all that dogs the weary lobsterman. Oil spills plague him. Trawlers, tankers, seiners, tugs and other large vessels, carelessly navigated, tear up his traps. Poachers raid them. One frustrated pound operator complains of the military brass and political bigwigs who fly into Maine at government expense, gather up and fly out with as much as a ton of live lobster at a clip. Not only does it deplete the meager supply, it often allows many of the lobsters to die in transit because of ignorance in handling them.

Right now live lobsters in Portland stores are $3.50 a pound. In Boston the price is $4.29. It takes seven lobsters to yield a pound of solid body meat, which sells for $11 to $12. Rather than ask their customers to pay what they believe to be outrageous prices, seafood restaurants in many areas have removed lobster specialties from their menus.

The lobster fisherman gets $2.00 to $2.25 a pound, but the work is grueling and the lobsters are scarce. You'd think a man who risks his life daily to bring in this delicacy deserves a chance once in a while to treat his own family to a lobster feed. Perhaps he does, once in a while, but it must be hard swallowing. Clothes for the kids, a few new traps, a replacement clutch for the old marine motor, all go to the dump along with the empty lobster shells.

So they eat beans, and this is as good a place as any to talk about beans. The Saturday night supper of home-baked beans and brown bread is traditional in Maine. Beans today come in cans and so does the brown bread. But a surprising number of Maine people still prepare them the old-fashioned way: the beans oven-baked in an earthenware pot with brown sugar, molasses, an onion and spices, and a chunk of salt pork; the brown bread made with sour milk, cornmeal, molasses and graham flour, steamed in a tightly covered lard bucket. Red kidney beans are the most popular. Other bean buffs swear by Jacob's cattle, yellow-eye and pea beans. No matter. I've sat down to perhaps two hundred town and church suppers in the last twenty-five years, and I've never tasted a dish of beans I didn't enjoy.

Side dishes run to a variety of slaws, salads and pickles, made from a family or neighbor's treasured recipe (pronounced *receipt* and spelled *recite*). Dessert is often fruit or berries from the orchard or field, preserved in jars to last through the winter and spring; or fresh Baldwin apples picked just before the first frost and kept down cellar in the coldest corner. A slab of "rat cheese," the tangy and mellow cheddar sliced from huge wheels on the meat counter of any village store, is the ideal companion to the apples. Gingerbread, hermits, molasses cookies, cakes with frostings and apple, blueberry, custard, rhubarb, chocolate cream and squash pies are not unknown.

Hot mince pie made with venison is an old and revered early morning standby for the men who go out in the dark of a cold morning to feed the livestock. Nothing sticks to the ribs better, they'll tell you, than hot mince pie on a frosty morning.

What's left in the bean pot after Saturday's supper is warmed up for Sunday's breakfast and served with a slab or two of hot apple pie and coffee. And warmed again and again until it's gone, say by Thursday noon, just in time for the pot to be scraped and scrubbed and washed and ready for next Saturday night's batch.

A steaming pot of chunky lobster stew with a fistful of crisp commons, a civilized version of hardtack or sea biscuit, crunched in over the floating lump of yellow country butter, would be a welcome treat of a Saturday night. But the way prices are, right now in March of 1972, the less said about lobster, the better.

108

THE PREDATORS

Man is mankind's worst predator. He kills more wantonly for sport than survival. Maine, being a last refuge of natural things like birds, mammals and fish, holds a powerful attraction for their pursuers. Today in Maine like everywhere else the old sports complain about the present poor state of bloodletting. " 'T ain't like it used to be," they growl. They rarely ask themselves why.

Maine does its best to protect the resident wildlife. It punishes poachers. It limits hunting and fishing seasons to reasonable periods. Deer hunting in the mid-season of 1971 was cut short, almost without warning, when the daily reports from inspection stations revealed a shockingly high kill at a time when the deer herd proved to be smaller than earlier estimates had indicated.

Insecticides are prohibited where they damage wildlife. Ecology is the freshest word in the litany of the New Environmentalists, a quasi-religious group whose concepts are sweeping the country. We try. Oh yes, we try hard.

Remember the caribou? Caribou disappeared from Maine about fifty years ago, preferring Canada to mass decimation. A few years ago the state swapped some of its partridge (ruffed grouse, really) for a herd of Newfoundland caribou and turned the caribou loose. With a few exceptions, they haven't been seen since.

We protect the moose. Maine's moose, like the giraffe, must be seen to be believed. I have watched a moose step over a six-foot snow fence as though it were a folded lawn chair. Moose are fearless. In the rutting season, a moose will charge a moving car head on.

Magnificent to observe, the moose, particularly when he's headed in some other direction. Game laws protect the moose. Yet moose meat is available anywhere in the state where a poacher can get off a few shots out of the game warden's hearing. There's talk of taking the law off moose. It would be a tragic mistake and the moose, like the caribou, would leave us. Smart animals like the timber wolf, panther and catamount left long ago. So did the wild swan and the wild turkey.

I got to thinking about wild turkeys. I had stumbled into a flock of them once in the lush woods of Matheson Hammock in Florida, years ago. It was an exciting experience for a woods buff accustomed to game birds no bigger than partridge. Had they disappeared from Maine's woods to go south for the winter? Or for keeps?

John Kimball of Cape Elizabeth suggested a chat with Amos Achorn. Achorn is a game bird breeder from way back. I decided to go. Hearing a name like Amos Achorn—pronounced *acorn*— how could I resist?

Amos works at the state game preserve and farm near Gray. He came from Canada to Maine and spent much of his life on the Holly Farm near Pemaquid, working for Milton Kimball and then for Roy Hollis of the *New York Times*. Amos took care of the sheep and Jersey cattle and the commercial raising of pheasants. Pheasants? I had come to talk about wild turkeys, but turkeys could wait. The "commercial" pheasant business had a nasty ring to it. How could anyone who loved wildlife raise those beautiful creatures just to destroy them by the hundreds and sell them for profit?

Amos explains. "No different from chickens. If we didn't raise 'em in captivity, they'd be long gone. Not only from poachers. There's fox, fisher cat, 'coon. They rob the nests of eggs. And like the hawks and owls they'll carry off the full-grown bird himself." He reminisced about the days back at Holly Farm in the 1940s. The farm was officially licensed to raise the birds, and metal tags were provided for the shipping and gift packaging of each brace of pheasants. At Thanksgiving and Christmas time, it was a thriving business. The birds were raised in pens and fed on the choicest game and turkey feed, until their time came. They were dressed out and put up in handsome gift packages, the box lined with spruce and fir boughs and decorated with bayberry and partridge berries. A package of wild rice or cranberry jelly was tucked between the bird's feet. Tied with a wide red ribbon and a big bow, the package, no higher than three inches and as long as the cock pheasant from beak to the tip of his splendid tail feathers, was shipped to pheasant fanciers all over the United States.

Amos has been with the state game farm at Gray since 1949. Thousands of pen-raised pheasants are released in different areas around the state well before the fall shooting season opens. It takes three to four weeks after captivity, Amos explains, for the tame pheasants to become "scarey." It's supposed to be time enough to give them a chance to grow wild before the first day of hunting.

Some chance. After confined pen raising and the daily presence of gamekeepers and feeding by tourists, most of the pheasants are as tame as yard chicks. The game farm uses a pickup truck, which goes down the long rows of pens with feed. Later, when the pheasants are freed in the woods and fields, the friendly sound of a motor brings them running to any car, jeep or truck. A shooting gallery or a firing squad couldn't offer a better setup for murder. What the hunters don't kill, the winter predators do. The fox and the owl and the frost.

Wild turkeys, *alors.*

They were slaughtered, is what happened, Amos says. But meanwhile he is looking smug and grinning and we are walking down to a set of pens apart and quite different from the pheasant pens. "Some years back," says Amos, "the Windham Rod and Gun Club give us two hens and a tom. Come spring of seventy-one and them hens laid twenty-one eggs and thirteen of 'em hatched good. Two weeks later, outta twenty-eight eggs, twenty-five hatched. Outta the whole lot, twenty-one survived and are doin' real good."

I looked at Amos' new breed of Maine wild turkeys. They look healthy and feisty, though compared to the supermarket toms, somewhat lean in the drumstick.

Amos points out it was a private project, not state-sponsored. They have released a few of the turkeys who promptly show up in farmers' dooryards, not wild yet by any means. They range long distances, Amos says, and for a long time to come, the law will have to be on them.

I say good-by to Amos and his not-yet-wild turkeys. I wonder how soon it will be until they're into the puckerbrush and deep woods of their primeval days, gobble-gobbling the chipmunks and squirrels out of their nut-pickin' minds.

If Amos Achorn and the rod and gun clubs have anything to do or say about it, it won't be long.

JOURNAL NOTE: City man came to Maine. First visit. Loved it. Bought himself a sightly view. Rounded up a country carpenter. Got himself a big city architect to draw up the plans. Mailed them to the carpenter. Told him to get to work at once and build the place. He'd be back the first of May, ready to move in. Couldn't wait. Phoned the carpenter in February.

"How's my house coming along?"

" 'T ain't."

"Roof's not up?"

"Nothin's up, mister."

"Damn it, why *not?*"

"That arch-a-teck feller is why not."

"What do you mean?"

"He didn't use you too good."

"Ridiculous! He's the best there is."

"His plans ain't."

"What's wrong with the plans?"

"Well, just for openers, mister, he got the bathroom in two different places."

You don't go to Lubec (Pop. 2,684) unless you really want to. If you're heading for Campobello Island, you have to. It means leaving U.S. 1 at Whiting and driving all the way back to Whiting when your visit is over.

Lubec has the usual waterfront and sardine factories and smoked herring sheds typical of the region. The candy-striped lighthouse at Quoddy Head State Park is on the

easternmost point of land in the United States. Tides here are the highest anywhere in the country, the rise and fall varying from twenty-seven feet down to twelve, with the average at 18.1 feet. Other advertised points of interest are a cove called Bailey's Mistake, named for a sea captain who put in here thinking it was Passamaquoddy Bay; and Raven Gulch, a narrow slot which puts on a spectacular display of smashing fountains of sea. But there's no road to Raven Gulch and it's no place for children or high heels. You can also climb a hilltop and see Eastport and Campobello and the outlying islands.

So much for Lubec's tourism. Disneyland it ain't. But Lubec has an unadvertised historic landmark worth the trip many times over. His name is Sumner T. Pike. Lubec born. Past eighty. Unmarried. Cleaned up in Wall Street in the thirties. Took it home to Lubec and sat on it.

A tall rumpled man, vigorous and articulate, with the visual impact of Dr. Spock crossed with Bernard Baruch. An impressive natural resource. I checked out his track record. Business advisor to the U. S. Secretary of Commerce. Member, Securities Exchange Commission, Atomic Energy Commission, Chairman of the Maine Public Utilities Commission . . .

". . . but why Lubec, sir?"

"Why not? My parents, all my grandparents and a few of my great-grandparents were born here. It's nothing for me to be here. This is Pike country."

Pike is chairman of the board of directors of a really strange organization called the Lubec Oceanographic Centre. Its stationery claims the centre is devoted to the study of the ocean and other liquids. It has a Lubec post office box number, an office at 2 Church Street (which turns out to be the Pike residence) and a study period daily from 5–6 P.M. The centre's motto is "All Chiefs, no Injuns." Advisors are welcome. I see shelves of books but no scientific marine equipment.

I note there are six members of the board of directors, five of whom are named Pike. Sumner, Moses, Alger, Radcliffe, Carleton. The sixth member, George McCurdy, is a Pike, being married to Sumner's sister. If Carleton's name had been Thomas or Timothy, the total Pike initials would spell out S.M.A.R.T. Most apt. Pikes are damned smart. Of good Maine root stock. Grew up smart, took off, ranged the world, struck it rich and, still smart, came home. All of them.

"Why?"

"It would be difficult to define it. I must say for myself I've lived away from here from about the time I went off to college until I came back from the Atomic Energy Commission. That was in 1951. In all that time I never got over the feeling that I was sort of camping out. I never felt I permanently belonged in the area in which I was living. It's hard to explain why a plant is where it is, except that's where its roots are."

"The Pike names interest me. Are they family names?"

"Mine is, in a way. My middle name, Tucker, is my mother's name. Sumner? Well, Alexander Baker Sumner lived here. He was a colonel in the Civil War. And my father's favorite gunning companion, was Sumner Stewart. Moses is an old family name. There's been seven Moses' here since we came over. In Alger's case one of Grandfather's sisters married a man named Alger French and he was named for this Alger. Radcliffe, well Radcliffe was pure invention. Radcliffe College had just gotten its name and my mother thought it was a good name and she gave it to him."

"You worked with Robert Oppenheimer in AEC. What was he like?"

"Brilliant. I remember when the general advisory committee got together and we were going to elect a chairman. Robert couldn't get to the meeting because of the weather and somebody suggested we elect Robert. He couldn't refuse because he wasn't there. Robert got there and the meeting got started. Robert took no notes. None at all, and we were covering some pretty complicated and delicate matters. Kind of worried me. Then when the time came to review and sum up, Robert sort of closed his eyes and put his fingers together. You'd think he was half dreaming. But when he was through talking, his summary was such that I don't recall ever a word being changed from the verbal or the written record. You could even tell where the commas came, from the way he spoke."

"Do you feel he was given a fair shake in those security investigations in 1954?"

"Well, the only people really interested in—persecuting or prosecuting—Robert, as far as I know, never changed their minds. Dear old Hickenlooper died very recently. I think he meant well but he had that Cedar Rapids, Iowa, mentality which is more than Puritan. It was transplanted from New England and got sourer and sourer. Lewis Strauss, the others, none of them changed their minds that I know of. Most of us felt Robert had been unfairly treated. He had a certain mental elegance. He grew up mentally very quickly, politically very, very late. He didn't sow his political wild oats like most kids do in their early twenties. He did his in his thirties, in California. But by the time Robert was picked by General Groves, the head of Alamos, I think he'd had it. I never questioned his love of country. I tried to tell those guys once, that if there was anything moral in the doctrine of atomic power, then it would seem to me any small errors and mistakes Robert made in the thirties were more than compensated for by the magnificent job he had done at Alamos in the development of the weapons."

"What about the atomic energy plants proposed for the Maine coast?"

"Of all the places available, I feel the Maine coast is probably the most suitable for a nuclear plant. Except for one thing. It isn't near a market. It can be costly getting electricity to a big market. But we do have the cold water and a strong set of tides and currents, so there's a very quick exchange. You don't run the danger of overheating the surrounding area to the point that it will affect the living environment. Our Maine coast water is never higher than sixty degrees and down to the thirties and forties in the winter. Experiments at Cousins Island were run testing how lobsters and crabs work under a certain degree of warmth. The best advice I can get from biologists and atomic geniuses who should know something about it, is that warmth would improve the piscatorial and the ecological life more than it would hurt it."

"Will it affect the shrimp draggers or herring seiners?"

"When you get out as far as the draggers work, I doubt it. Close to shore — well, Bob Dow's the best man in our fisheries division. Bob feels very strongly that the temperature all along the Maine coast has been too cold for the ideal development of lobsters. He's got quite a lot of evidence to back him up. It slows the growth. Apparently there's some optimum temperature which may be, let's say, fifty-seven. For the last several years it's been dropping. The growth of the lobsters, according to the biologists, has slowed down.

"Clams, for example. The water here at Eastport and Lubec is ten degrees colder than down west at Casco Bay, and it takes the clams twice as long to grow to the commercial minimum size. A properly designed atomic plant, properly located and operated along this coast, with the higher temperatures it would give the water, would probably do our oceanographic population more good than harm."

Pike's feelings are mixed on the establishment of a proposed oil refinery in Eastport. But they aren't mixed equally. "I'd hate to see us going all out for a polluting industry, yet I don't like being dependent on three months a year tourism and little else. This gets way down to the gizzard of things. I do hope we can work out some sort of a medium course. We can have occupations for our local people that aren't degrading. By and large, serving tourists is degrading. I'm an Eastport taxpayer because of property there and I'd like to see better schools and lower taxes. But as a resident of Lubec and a taxpayer here I'd be opposed to an oil refinery because of the potential pollution and almost no tax benefits."

Pike admits there would be navigational risks in bringing supertankers into Eastport. Even though refinery techniques have been improved, minor spills must be expected. Acquiring the fossil fuel to power our technology has become a critical problem and may well develop into a terminal case. It took millions of years to create the oil and coal we've burned up in just the last fifty years.

"Over half of it," Pike says, "was consumed in the last twenty-five or thirty years. We're using more of it than we find each year and the price of it piles higher and higher. We can't produce all we need and we can't find all we need. And the people in the places where oil is most plentiful have gotten rich and powerful and they're telling us we can have the oil on their terms now, instead of on ours."

"What about pollution in the rest of Maine?"

"It's a struggle all right. One of our jobs is to go back and clean up the mess we've allowed to happen in our rivers and our air. I think we're well on our way. The awareness of and reaction to pollution has surprised me, how fast it's come on since I was first in the Legislature. You couldn't get a bill by, then. I remember our bill to clean up the rivers. It was written beautifully, until you got right down to it. Excepted from that bill were the Saco, Androscoggin, Kennebec, Penobscot and St. Croix rivers. Joe Sewall worked damned hard on it though it went against the interests of some of his best customers. I feel we're making progress and we're going to make more. The cleanup jobs are going

to be very expensive but that's part of the future of Maine. Tremendous costs are almost inevitable for the big saltwater harbors along the coast but it's necessary. It's necessary to have not only the strictest of regulations *before,* but the strictest of enforcement *afterward.* You don't get strict regulations if the people doing the polluting are paying the inspectors. You've got to have a completely dedicated, completely independent crowd to do the job. And this can be very difficult."

I ask Pike about the mysterious Lubec Oceanographic Centre.

"Years ago when I was appointed to the Oceanographic Committee of the National Academy of Sciences, we held our first meeting in Washington. We sat around a table with all our sponsors. Those were the guys who had put up the money but they didn't know what they had put it up *for,* or who we were. Harrison Brown from CalTech was chairman and began introducing everyone, starting from the left. These were all eminent scientific people from famous institutions. Except me, of course. When he came to me, I was introduced as Sumner Pike, Lubec Oceanographic Centre. Well, it cleared the atmosphere and I was very happy about my promotion. First thing I did when I got home, I had the local paper feller draw up a letterhead and under the fancy title it said *Invented November 15, 1958 by Harrison Brown.*"

"Is it still an active organization?"

Pike smiles. "Well, you know how it is. A few of the boys get together . . ."

JOURNAL NOTE: Two years ago, Mrs. Rita Willey of Rockland packed sixty-seven cans full of 536 sardines in eight minutes and became the world's fastest sardine packer of the year. Mrs. Willey represented the North Lubec Canning Company in the packing contest, the first world championship ever held. She was determined to win again, but was defeated last year by Mrs. Patricia Havener of East Friendship, Maine. The new world's champion sardine packer packed ninety cans in ten minutes, beating Mrs. Willey by four cans. Mrs. Willey, who is pretty and has four children, did not go to the Olympics and she wasn't invited to the White House. But she did make the local news and wire services and went to New York and appeared on three national TV shows.

"I was working on just nerves," she says. Mrs. Willey knows her herrings, which is what sardines really are. With eight to a can, she explains, it's easy; only the heads are snipped. But the herring catch lately is bringing in a larger variety and they pack four to a can. "You have to snip both head and tail," Mrs. Willey says, "and the bigger ones are harder to handle."

This year, Rita Willey recaptured her crown. Eighty-five cans in ten minutes.

Hope for the preservation of Maine's natural beauty has been bolstered by the creation of a state Environmental Improvement Commission with authority to veto industrial sites that threaten the Maine image. A proposal to build a $150 million oil installation on Sears

Island in Penobscot Bay has met tough opposition from sources other than environmental commissions and outraged citizens. Opposition like Ossie Beal.

Ossie is pure Yankee, slow-speaking, bedenimed, reassuring to look at in his red and black zippered buffalo wool plaid. Beals have lobstered and fished and built boats and raced them in and around Penobscot Bay since Maine's infancy. Ossie heads the Maine Lobstermen's Association and is opposed to oil refineries for practical reasons having nothing to do with the esthetics or ecology of the area. More than a thousand licensed lobstermen work 180,000 traps in the bay, worth a bit over two million dollars each year.

"Even with oil spills," Ossie says, ". . . it's well known and will be attested to by any lobster fisherman, that ships, barges and tugs do great damage to lobster traps by cutting off the buoys and toggles."

Beal doesn't waste words. He studied the navigation courses proposed by the oil refinery group and in their plans discovered the lack of ballast that would make for light incoming barges. He's discussed the situation at length with fishermen who would be affected by this traffic, men who work their traps from Deer Isle to Stonington to the east, and Monhegan Island to the west. "Winds and tides will often carry the empty barges well to starboard or port of the tug pulling them. The hawser, moving at angles to the course, will act almost like a mine sweeper, clipping off toggles and buoys in their path."

Eastport, Sears Island—the controversy rages on. Residents, fishermen, summer visitors and the entire gamut of Audubon-oriented conservationists regard the oil companies as so many villainous predators intent only on ravaging and despoiling Maine's lovely seacoast for personal gain. On the obverse side are those who couldn't care less for the looks of the place as long as there are jobs and a much needed cash flow of business activity. Someone's got to do something and do it soon.

Maine's governor, Kenneth M. Curtis, is in the middle, damned if he does and damned if he doesn't. Young and capable, Curtis is a country boy himself. He agrees strongly that Maine's natural beauty must be preserved and protected. He also believes such protection and preservation is not necessarily incompatible with the healthy economic growth the state sorely needs.

He is particularly aware of his responsibility for the welfare of his people. Economically, Maine is a poor state. Its industries—pulp and paper, food, leather and textiles—promise little hope for a booming expansion. Unemployment in Maine runs higher than the average across the nation and especially high (over 12 per cent) in Washington County, a prime target for the oil boys. Curtis' arguments are as hardheaded as Ossie Beal's.

"You can't plow roads or keep the schools open without tax money. How are you going to clean up the environmental damage that's already been done? That will certainly occur in the future? A lot of those people who oppose oil projects in Maine are people from other states who have made their money polluting other states and now they've come here for serenity. The only solution for Maine, a solution that will give our people their equal share of the nation's wealth and with it a chance to live decently, free of oppressive economic pressures, is to encourage and promote and develop industry here, but only those industries that are compatible with the environment."

JOURNAL NOTE: I was driving north in what Steinbeck calls "the silver chill of a Maine afternoon." Rounding a bend in the road from Machias to Calais I caught a flash of movement about a hundred yards ahead at the shoulder of the road. Some creature—nothing small—had crossed the road and disappeared from sight.

I slowed but would not have stopped except for another flurry of movement in the brush. I cut the motor twenty yards away and studied the thick ground cover of ferns and puckerbrush. Nothing moved. I got out and approached cautiously. Something moved just once, convulsively. Partridge? Pheasant? Too large for that, I guessed. I could see nothing. All was still.

I picked up a length of crooked tree limb. "Popple," it's called. I inched closer. In the coarse gravel at the road's edge, two drops of blood glistened. I gripped the stick tightly and reaching out, carefully lifted back the heavy fern growth.

At once with a terrible thrashing, a huge bird rose from the depths of its hiding place and faced me squarely. Fierce-eyed, open-beaked, a young eagle. Golden, bald, I could not know. I swear now I heard a hissing. One enormous dark wing spread out and upward. The other, the left one, sagged, broken. I could see where the bullet had creased a swift cruel path through wing and breast, where feathers were splashed and flecked with sunlight and scarlet.

I dared not move. Its fierce presence held me rooted. The stick? I lowered it. Help was needed, not violence again.

Help how? Enough strength remained in those talons to rake flesh to ribbons. Two sweeps of the curved beak could tear eyes from sockets.

It took an effort for me to back away, so mesmeric was the encounter. So full of pity was I, unable to help and my heart bitter with anger for his destroyer.

I drove slowly past the deep green that covered him. All still again. Dead, perhaps. Nothing.

Farther north the road passes through Cobscook State Park and the heart of the Moosehorn National Wildlife Refuge. Havens. Sanctuaries. We try. We really do. I would find a ranger and report it. But where, in this wilderness? And why, now that the damage was done? It would soon be dark. I continued sore in spirit to my destination.

Few eagles are left in Maine. Fewer now.

123

THE PRESENT PAST

Portland is Maine's major city. It's a seaport, a trade and distribution center. Since the mid-nineteenth century it has maintained an unusually high level of cultural activity. Although its population (64,300 in the 1970 census) dropped 12.5 per cent in the past decade, perimeter towns like Cape Elizabeth, Cumberland, Falmouth, Gorham, Westbrook and Yarmouth have grown in population, indicating that people in Maine, like everywhere else in America, are shifting from city to country living.

In the arts, performing and visual, Portland is best known for its musical endeavors. The Portland Symphony, directed by Paul Vermel, performs in the City Hall auditorium which, in 1968, was given a remarkable interior face-lifting. Leonard Nelson, an attorney and past board of trustees president of the Symphony Association, was one of several people influential in bringing it to its artistically and financially healthy state. He's also chairman of the state's Commission on the Arts and the Humanities.

"Portland is not about to become the center of the western art world," Nelson says, "but it is a remarkably vivacious hub of regional artistic pursuits. Our symphony concerts outdraw boxing and wrestling. Our drama, music and literary groups are steadily expanding their audiences. We have a highly talented and widely known community of coastal painters who exhibit and sell in Portland and elsewhere.

"The rest of Maine is distinguished by enormous individual rather that institutionalized effort. Maine isn't known to be highly innovative and it's unlikely to develop any startling new art forms. But we're free of the constraints of urban centers. Maine craftsmen can take the time to produce excellent work. We have a solid reputation for creating well-made worthwhile things. It's an inspiring heritage for our young people and we take pride in it."

The city of Portland seems to inch, cobble by cobble, brick by brick, into the twentieth century. For some Portlanders this represents too swift and violent a change. For others it's a hopeless drag. My own feelings are mixed. I cherish the old. The new intrigues and stimulates me.

The east end of Monument Square, the downtown hub, was originally occupied by the old United States Hotel and then taken over and remodeled by Edwards & Walker, a rambling, multipartite emporium dealing in hardware and sporting goods. In spite of endemic confusion and an apathetic sales force, the store had an undeniable charm and fascination and was held in great affection by its customers. Its inventory spanned the needs of country and farm since mid-nineteenth century. I could always pick up a handle for an outdated pump, a dasher for the old White Mountain ice cream hand freezer (which I still use), a spare blade for the bucksaw or a few wooden spiles for drawing off maple sap.

Edwards & Walker quit the retail business and the building some years ago and moved to a new location, where it serves only wholesale customers. Now I go to Longley's in Norway, praying each yard of the sixteen-mile drive it hasn't gone the way of Edwards & Walker.

When they tore down the Monument Square landmark to make way for the Casco Bank's ten-story office building, the workingmen were astonished to find vestiges of the half-forgotten hotel with room partitions and wash basins and the coach and carriage courtyard still intact.

The Casco Bank office building was the first major construction job in Portland since 1925. A burst of feverish building activity followed. A new motel is carving a huge slice out of the city's midsection. Only by the skin of its boards and battens and a last-minute grant of funds was a priceless Gothic Revival dwelling saved from the swinging ball of the demolishers and moved to a site more suitable to its grace and distinction.

Like cities everywhere, Portland must pay a heavy price to solve its traffic problems. A wide swath of the new Interstate 295 spur gouges its path across the city, skirting Back Cove. In one swipe it leveled a couple of hundred years of familiar landscape and landmarks. Plans for shopping centers, downtown malls and more motels, all in the name of progress, provide a poor prognosis for the status quo.

Portland is a treasure house of eighteenth- and nineteenth-century architectural ingenuity and styling. The surviving structures and artifacts of these periods, the wood, stone and metal detailings, comprise a rare and irreplaceable heritage. In spite of areas of urban blight, the city still offers lovely vistas and streetscapes.

In his introduction to *PORTLAND*, a recent publication of Greater Portland Landmarks, the Boston historian and author Walter Muir Whitehill says of Portland, "It has a human scale and pleasing variety . . . It is blessedly free of the monotony of Manhattan Island or of cities set in a boundless prairie . . . I have come to the city on and off for thirty-five years, and can still wander its streets with pleasure."

I wonder what it must have been like growing up in a plain honest New England town like Portland and I ask Jane Moody, who's lived most of her life here. (She was Jane McLane Smith then. Now she's Mrs. William Moody and works hard for the landmarks preservation group.) Her great-great-grandfather came over the mountains from New Hampshire in 1798 and eventually settled on a Hanover farm near Rumford. His oldest son took off for Portland one day and settled. His descendants have been around here since.

Jane's first memories center around the old Union Station (demolished several years ago for a shopping center) and the overnight State of Maine express that brought her over the bumpy rail bed from New York. She speaks of the drive through Deering's Oaks to Falmouth for the summer.

"It was always early morning, always June and always a beautiful perfect day. Later of course we moved up here year round to be brought up, educated and sent off again to make our own paths."

Growing up for Jane Smith of Portland, Maine, meant sailboats, stacks of books, plenty of woods to walk or ride in with no sounds of civilization.

"Do you know that we actually canoed? And on the bay only? In the early spring or fall when the wind was too cold on the bay for sailing, we'd spend hours paddling ourselves up Mill Creek, always thinking we'd find its source before the tide turned and ran out. Riding the tide out was one thing. Missing it meant a long, muddy, dragging hike. Abandoning the canoe for later retrieval was unthinkable.

"The bay was a large part of our lives. Out of bed and into the sailboats and off to explore three hundred and sixty-five islands and Portland harbor—that was the daily summer fare. Mackerel Cove to the east, Hussey Sound and the ship channel to the south, were our boundaries. The rest except for the Navy was pretty much our private playground."

The summer would pass with venturesome sailing up Fore River or the other way to Harpswell, which took some planning so that the long trip back would not wind up in back-breaking paddling to get home before dark. Racing the boats was a special treat, giving the all-girl crew a certain cachet.

Wintertime meant skiing on neighborhood hills straight down and walking up. "Wooden skis," Jane recalls, "and *real bindings,* please. Twice a winter we had a trip to North Conway and the skimobile. Up at dawn, 'ambulance money' in our pockets and the milk train to Montreal at six-thirty A.M. From Union Station, of course. The 'ambulance money' was never spent and we'd be home by eight P.M.

"By the time the war was over our lives had changed. High school almost finished, blackouts lifted, gas in the car, and college—or no college—decisions to be made. Sunbathing became a cosmetic necessity and one day, quite suddenly, we were no longer children."

Jane Moody's involvement with landmarks preservation sharpens her concern for Portland's future look:

"'Cobble by cobble, brick by brick . . .' I like the phrase but I fear it. I see all sorts of walls come tumbling down. Many are tumbling and perhaps many should. It's my impression the twentieth century has been most unkind to cities. Many are increasingly unlivable, choked with traffic, split by arterials, crime-ridden and ghetto-pocked. Brick by brick, sure. But let's make the twentieth century work here. Let's not repeat the Bayonnes and Baltimores by adopting the worst the century has to offer."

Portland architect A. Holmes Stockly makes no bones about his feelings. "For a long time," he says, "Portland society and politics permitted city developers to do as they pleased and what they did was less from civic pride than selfish motivation. Now the people who have control are finding out there are better ways of doing things. What we have here is worthwhile. The city is full of buildings of fine quality and a lot of care was given them. This is one of the jobs of preservation Landmarks has been trying to do. We must persuade these people that putting up shoddy and ill-conceived structures simply defeats the purpose. Someone has got to give them the right options of good contemporary design that still reflects the traditional heritage so that the infill will continue the original character of the city."

I stroll up Munjoy Hill and swing down around Oxford Street. Much has to be done and some undone. Where slum structures were leveled modern ticky-tacky now stands, no better except for the plumbing than the eyesore it replaced. What is missing and what the good misguided city cries out for is an awareness of its identity with a distinguished past. Given good planning and empathic owners and architects and above all the love of the people for the honest look of their place, the transition will restore pride to the city and fulfill the dreams of those who love it.

The air is brisk and clean. The good Maine air. The streets are quiet this Sunday morning and there are skaters on the pond in Deering's Oaks. I watch them from my car, admiring and envious on the curving drive. A chubby eight-year-old swathed in a wool scarf and gloves and leggings takes a spill. No one moves to help her. Rump high she struggles up, puffing and shrieking and skates off shaky but undaunted. The skaters — there aren't many — follow no traffic pattern as they do in Rockefeller Plaza's posh skating rink. These are Maine folk. They take a pratfall now and then. Get up. Go their independent way.

TASTE OF MEMORY

Dorris Isaacson probably knows as much about the state of Maine as anyone. Back in the Depression she took over the stalled Federal Writers Project and produced the first Maine Down East guide in 1937. She has been involved in the state's historical and cultural affairs for more than thirty years. In 1971 a revised edition of the Maine guide appeared, updated and with many new photographs. The editor: Dorris Isaacson.

Referring to Maine then and now as reflected in those volumes, she says: "In taking an overview of life in Maine again after thirty years, one becomes more acutely aware of changing times and tempo. Unless you have lived through a general depression you cannot appreciate the atmosphere and temper of the 1930's when time seemed suspended in the paralyzed economy. Without work and in need of life's bare necessities, great numbers of Americans came to know numbing poverty, bitter despair and the humiliation of the relief rolls.

"Beautiful Maine was indeed Vacationland — but those with mouths to feed had other things on their minds besides the scenery and the preservation of heritage and environment. Like the pioneers, their concern was survival. I remember one angry poetic comment on hunger versus aesthetics that did not appear in the guide — 'you and your goddam autumn twilight.'

"Republican Maine did not suffer gladly FDR's make-work WPA projects, particularly those concerned with 'culture' which were regarded askance as a real boondoggle. As Dorothy Parker wrote, actors, artists, authors and such 'never know nothing and never know much' — those on the Federal Arts Projects were sort of the flower children of the Thirties. But they, too, had to eat. So what began as make-work evolved into the beginnings of popular interest in America's cultural heritage. The first in-depth portrait of the American people, produced in the forty-eight state guides by the Federal Writers Project, has proved of lasting value. Although there were no Conrad Aikens or Vachel Lindsays on the Maine project, the assembled talents developed an esprit de corps and pride of crafts-manship that meant more than a meal ticket via government handout. Beginning with some 200 people of all ages, the project wound up with a dozen. Long before the book was finished—it took over two years—Washington began ordering staff cutbacks. It wasn't easy to let people go. They had nowhere to turn. They had to go on welfare. One girl's alternative was suicide. I recall receiving simultaneous telegrams from two Washington departments: '1000 words on Tour 1 for Monday' and 'Release 10 staffers by Monday.' My response: 'No workers, no copy.'

"But it wasn't all grim. In what was perhaps the camaraderie of adversity in more innocent times, there was generosity, compassion, humor and gaiety even if you didn't know where your next meal was coming from. . . . You learned a lot about humanism in those days. Perhaps we again need to learn more of humanism as we confront the complex problems of the 1970's, not necessarily in the breadlines, but in seeking to improve the quality of life."

A Lewiston native of English-Scottish descent, Dorris Isaacson succinctly epigraphs her biography: Baptist-born, convent-bred, kosher bride. Growing up in the Jazz Age of John Held, Jr., *College Humor* and early Hemingway, she spent summers at Robinhood where her mother, an art teacher in the Maine school system, studied with William Zorach. From convent studies in literature, drama and music, she went directly into newspaper work at the Lewiston *Journal,* society and obituaries at $12 a week.

"Those were the days of on-the-job training, so to speak. Busy editors took a dim view of journalism school graduates who had to be re-trained for practical purposes. Newspaper-ing then seemed romantic and glamorous—but not from the society desk. How to breach the then male preserve of general news, the human drama of the courtroom, crime, politics, etc. . . .

"The chance came when I replaced two men in the Lewiston office of the Portland *Evening News,* a democratic paper that, under the editorship of Ernest L. Gruening (who subsequently headed the Department of the Interior and later was Governor and U.S. Senator, Alaska), for a time fought the 'power interests' in Maine. Also, work as a stringer for New York and Boston papers and *Time* magazine was useful experience in the male world where I must say I was made to feel like a newspaperman, not a sob sister confined to the 'woman's angle.' There were a few newsbeats such as Democrat Louis J. Brann's gubernatorial candidacy (I was a staff aide during his terms of office), a labor interview with Henry Wallace that created a mild national flurry, crime investigation, radio coverage of floods and conflagrations and the like.

"After the *News* folded, came the Depression, and the Writers Project. About the time Senator Margaret Chase Smith was beginning her political career, I did a women-in-politics column for the Gannett papers. When male reporters' ranks were depleted during World War II, I became the first and so far only woman to handle state politics for the papers. This says something but I'm not sure what. At any rate, the new era of sophisticated news media as we know it today began soon after the war ended, offering greater challenges for trained specialists in an increasingly complex world."

Writer-editor of the national award-winning town history, *Phippsburg, Fair to the Wind,* Dorris Isaacson and her husband, whose avocations are world travel, live half the year in Phippsburg at the mouth of the Kennebec River, where the first attempted English settlement on the northern Atlantic coast was made in 1607. She continues her service of many years on various state commissions relating to Maine's culture and heritage and in 1971, received national and state awards in recognition of her work.

The community of Robinhood sits among hilly islands and coves at the edge of the sea. Dahlov and Adolph Ipcar live nearby on an old secluded farm close to the place where her artist parents lived and worked since 1922. Dahlov Ipcar's imaginative and colorful paintings and her books for children are sheer delight. This is the first opportunity I have had to spend time with her. She has a gentle quality when she speaks, a grace of mien.

I had just mentioned the unspoiled look of the country road on the run from U.S. 1 to the sea. Dahlov shakes her head. "They're planning to put a sixty-foot right of way on both sides of that road. It's a shame. Years back when they cut timber in these woods, they used to leave a protective stand of big trees close to the roadside. Now they'll be cutting those down. There'll be nothing left but second growth."

The year-round population on Georgetown Island, I'm told, is about five hundred. The heaviest development seems to be at Indian Point, where there are about seventy or so summer cottages.

"When we first came here," Dahlov says, "if you went out to the beach and one other family was there, you felt the beach was crowded."

The Ipcars came to stay year round in 1937, soon after they were married. They were determined to make it a working farm, to live off the land. They did.

"Hard physical labor can be very satisfying," Dahlov says quietly. "For years I went out and did all the farm work with my husband. I'd go out in the hay field and help bring in the hay and store it up in the barn. It made me feel I'd accomplished something worthwhile, getting our supply of hay in for the winter."

"Dahlov's a real farmhand," Adolph says, beaming.

"I still feel romantic about farming," she admits. "I think you've got to have some of this feeling in you or you'll never stand the grind of farm life. If you feel it's drudgery then you're miserable."

Adolph says, "Some of my friends feel romantic about farming and never succeed. They're too romantic, never serious enough about the hard work. Or practical enough to put in a sustained effort day after day right through the year."

Dahlov says, "If you're too romantic you don't really see what's happening. I mean, your hay is getting wet and you're out there admiring the beautiful flowers in some dell when you ought to be rushing to get the hay in. You have to have a practical sense about farming along with the feeling that it's a beautiful and worthwhile life."

Adolph begins to describe the dairy business he started in those days. "This milk peddling of mine was slow at first. We had only eight cows and the commercial dairies in Bath and Brunswick were serving the area. Ours was straight Jersey milk with the cream way down below the shoulder of the bottle and that really impressed the local people and created confidence in us. One old man loved my milk so much—he was about eighty—I said to him one time, 'You'd better be careful. The doctors are advising people not to consume too much butter fat.' He just glared at me and he said, 'Now, you mind your own business, young feller.'"

"We had the most beautiful milk in the world," Dahlov says, looking wistful.

What kind of reception did they have, being city people "from away" when they decided to live year round?

"Art was considered an absolute frill in the schools," Dahlov says. "It never occurred to people that someone could be an artist and be respectable. He was just a bum or a loafer. The feeling's changed lately. People are seeing that artists do work very hard and sometimes make money—very much like themselves. And they're seeing that art is used in all kinds of ways."

"They seem very proud of the artists in their towns around here," Adolph says. "I hear no talking down of artists."

What about the schools when their kids were growing up?

"We thought at first we'd live an isolated kind of life here," Dahlov says, "but when the children were ready to enter school our ideas changed very fast. The school system then consisted of two one-room schoolhouses, each manned by a very old lady. Each schoolhouse had forty to forty-five students and we knew something had to be done about improving education in the town."

It wasn't easy. The Ipcars together with other young parents in town talked with the school superintendent and the education department in Augusta. They agreed to try for a central school with a modern building and young, qualified teachers.

"We did it with our own town funds," Adolph recalls. "About a hundred and twenty-five children were involved. It called for a kindergarten and eight grades. We organized a PTA, feeling it could produce votes at the next town meeting. In six weeks we had over a hundred members, including some whose children were already grown up. We held a special town meeting and the new school went through, something like eighty-eight to twelve." He grins. "Those twelve said . . . 'what was good enough for us and our daddies was good enough for *your* children.' I told them I had a look at the old town reports and when their daddies went to school they had eleven schoolhouses in this town and now we only had two."

"They had something like six or seven children to a teacher then," Dahlov says.

Adolph served as chairman of the school board for nine years. After that he became

town moderator for the annual town meetings. He's held the job for the past fifteen years.

"You feel people have great trust in you if they give you that job. Our last town meeting had seventy articles. It started at ten in the morning and ended at six that night. A real grind."

The Ipcars, like so many coastal residents, have become deeply involved in the battle with the oil and atomic energy interests, fighting to preserve the natural unspoiled beauty of their region. I ask Dahlov if her work as an artist isn't being neglected because of these activities. She thinks about it for a moment. "Not at all. The way our life style is threatened makes it as necessary to act as does one's art involvement. Or farm involvement if one's a farmer. You do what has to be done."

We walk outside over hilly farmland and fields. The last trace of winter is gone from the earth. The apple trees look fragile in first bud. I leave in a while, feeling I have been with good people, decent people, who love the land, who give as much or more to life as they take from it.

Ellen Newell Tiemer lives in Cundy's Harbor but she grew up in Bath. "I remember the wintertime particularly," she says. "There were wooden sidewalks and with the first fall of snow you'd hear the *squeak squeak squeak* of people's feet going by. We used to have a great time hitching our sleds to a sleigh. It was a milk delivery sleigh or one for delivering groceries. We'd just be hauled all over town and end up miles away from home. It would be cold and dark and we'd hope to get a ride home, which we usually did. Another thing we did was skijoring. I think some of the kids do it these days, but it's a little hard with all the traffic around and not very snowy roads.

"During the summertime one of our great treats was to take a trolley car in Bath. We'd dress all up in our Sunday best, take the ride in an open trolley car from the north end to the south end and back to where we started. It was a big deal in those days. You couldn't get very far except by trolley.

"For my first Bowdoin house party I took the trolley car in 1922 from Bath and was met at the First Parish church in Brunswick. My sister, six years younger, said, 'I don't believe it!' It was the only way I had to get there. I arrived all dressed up with hat and cape. It was an Ivy House party, Memorial Day, May thirtieth. I can see my horrible rig then. I made all my own clothes. Being there with all those New York and Boston girls, I really felt like an old hick. I don't think I opened my mouth through the whole thing. I was only sixteen years old at the time. It was all a part of growing up."

I ask Ellen about the handsome nineteenth-century homes that line Bath's streets.

"They belonged mostly to the people who owned the wooden shipyards. There were at least fourteen shipyards in Bath alone and more down the Kennebec River. I think there were twenty-three in all. Fortunes were made on these ships. Not only building them, but the people who built them often had a share in the ships' trade and business was very

good in those days. Most of those houses you see were built from the money from the wooden shipbuilding days."

"When did the Newell family get into shipbuilding?"

"My father worked in Bath summers while he was at MIT. He came to Bath in 1902. He was a draughtsman. His family came from Winchester, Mass., but he acted more like a Maine native than my mother, who was born in Bath. He used to love to say, 'Down the rud a piece,' things like that. He married my mother in 1907. Her name was Carolyn Moulton."

"Do you call Bath or Cundy's Harbor your home?"

"Well, I'm glad to be here in Cundy's Harbor living on the water. Where we lived in Bath, we didn't really see the water. We were a little far away from it. I don't know very many people in Bath now. The place has changed, grown and what not. I'm really more concerned with Brunswick and the goings-on there. The college is close by. There's not much connection between Bath and Brunswick. There never has been. So now we're really more Brunswick-oriented. Because of the college, and most of our friends are there."

Ellen's husband, Paul, is a transplant from New Jersey. He enjoys Maine, he says. He attended Bowdoin and early in his business life set Maine as an objective.

"Most of the people we know here are ones who have been in Maine a good deal longer than I have. They have a set of values which I accept pretty well, whereas, living in the framework of sham where I formerly lived, commuting and working in New York, it was not satisfying."

Does he find Maine people more down-to-earth?

"I'd say that's it. They seem to place values, whether it's a boat, a car, a necktie or a person, pretty much on how it reacts on them, within themselves. It's the simplest and best way to make judgments."

No one defends the preservation of Maine's primordial image more fiercely than John Cole, editor of the weekly *Maine Times*. Let oil powers try a putsch, or errant snowmobilers violate the countryside's peace and privacy and John is in there snarling and growling them off before he chews them to bits. If snowflakes polluted, John would be up there having it out with the Lord Himself.

Tough guy? Not always; though a Cole editorial born of outrage for a righteous cause can make an acid bath seem by comparison less corrosive than a dose of salts. John's gentle (and true) nature reveals itself regularly on the opposite page in John's column — his escape hatch from the tensions of the watchdog vigil he keeps.

His prose reflects the journalist's wistful yearning for literary immortality. His recurring theme is nostalgia, ladled out with a sentimentality sometimes mushier than the spring thaw. But when he's good, he's damned good. At his best, he's downright lyrical.

Recently with a premature burst of springtime upon the land, John with an errand to run took the longest, most remote back roads to get where he was going. The journey left him shaken, he reports, and grieving for the skeletons of abandoned farms he saw along the way. ". . . the tumbled beams of a falling barn . . . the blackness of a gaping cellar hole; and on the buckled porches of the windowless gray buildings . . . the ghostly farm women walking with their day's wash on their arm, happy to have the warm sun to hang it in."

After a long hard Maine winter John sees the coming of spring as a medium conjuring up the spirits of departed farmers, begging their return to shore up sagging buildings, fix torn and leaking roofs, build fires in cold and rusted stoves, clear bull briars from barnyards, restore life and purpose to these once lovely, carefully crafted places.

"These gray and lonely farms were once the strength of Maine; now they are nothing but so much rotting wood, land gone fallow, homes without inhabitants . . . the pines are taking hold, slowly, the way people fill a church for the earliest service. Soon the trees will take all, and Maine will have forgotten the lives of dignity, independence and grace once lived on these fine farms."

In the autumn of 1971, the Maine Commission on the Arts and the Humanities gave an award to the Shaker community of Sabbathday Lake, New Gloucester.

The award comes as a somewhat melancholy ave to a passing people at a curious moment in our own state of social upheaval. The religious doctrine of Shakerism is firmly based in both the equality and the separation of the sexes. It does, however, go further into self-denial than some Women's Libbers care to go. Sexual intercourse is strictly prohibited. The vow of chastity is frankly and rigorously enforced. Shaker "families" consist of communal groups of men, women and children organized for the purpose of work and religious devotion.

What gives the substance of immortality to the Shaker tradition and cause for grief at the prospect of its fleshly demise, is the quality and spirit of its art and craftsmanship, its husbandry skills, its architectural purity. No task was too humble to merit the creation of perfect tools with which to do the job. Spareness created a functional elegance that dumbfounded and irritated the Victorians. Today these same Shaker lines delight the discerning eye.

The award was accepted on behalf of the Shakers by Sister Mildred Barker. George Tice and I had visited the Maine Shaker community and met Sister Mildred several months earlier. Seeing her at the awards luncheon warmed my heart and reawakened memories of that visit in May.

We were met by an affable young man named Theodore E. Johnson. He is the director of the Sabbathday Lake Museum. A catalogue published in 1969 by the Bowdoin College Museum of Art on the occasion of an exhibition of Shaker art, called *Hands to Work and Hearts to God,* contains along with more than forty fine photographs by John McKee an excellent essay on the Shaker tradition in Maine written by Mr. Johnson.

Mr. Johnson invites us to sit. He tells us there are only two Shaker communities left in the United States. Total population is seventeen women. Five make up the community in Canterbury, New Hampshire. The remainder are at Sabbathday Lake. There are no living men, boys or girls. Sister Frances Carr, an attractive brunette with sparkling eyes, is the world's youngest Shaker.

Brother Delmer Wilson, a noble spirit and respected craftsman, died in 1961. He was the last male survivor. Maine's first Shaker, circa 1783, was John Cotton of Alfred. His enthusiasm spread to enough Maine people to establish Shaker communities in Alfred, Gorham, Poland and New Gloucester.

Shaker landholdings at one time were extensive. The present site of the Poland Spring House is on original Shaker land on the farm of Gowen Wilson, one of the first converts. But the "families" dwindled. Hired hands were taken on to do the fieldwork. Now the cooper and blacksmith shops are gone, along with the carding, grist, saw and shingle mills. The school is shut down. There is no post office.

Mr. Johnson, who must leave, excuses himself and presents us to Sister Mildred Barker. She seems cautious at first. The community is the target of tourists from everywhere—some curious, some nosy. There's a difference, Sister Mildred explains pleasantly, and soon warms to the idea of our visit. We are invited to share the midday meal of soup, salad, homemade bread and preserves. It is absolutely delicious. I decide that if Shakers deny themselves some of the joys of living, they more than make up for it in others.

I suggest this discreetly to Sister Mildred. She explains that Shaker cookery, like everything else the Shakers turn hands and minds to, is a striving for human excellence. Everything done to perfection. Simplicity, she explains, is the keynote of the Shaker's religious belief—the natural simple love of God.

George wanders off to take pictures. I offer to help with the dishes but I'm turned down. I stroll with Sister Mildred for a few minutes in a nearby garden. George is setting up his tripod across the road. The harsh winter has split a forsythia bush. It blossoms in a hangdog way alongside its more robust sisters. I wonder if it will live or die. I wonder if it matters if one forsythia dies, when all around it a way of life dies.

A venerable willow like a silken-bearded mandarin is bowed and seems to be praying. For the sun? For the dead? Sister Mildred is watching me. She has a cheerful face and suddenly I'm warmed and I like her. In the distance of several hillsides the rigid towers of the Poland Spring House seem to wobble in the sky, a fading yellow Camelot.

We go inside, gathering in the hollow silence of the varnished hallways the honest smell of simmering herbs. I am strangely peaceful in this final place. Too bad, I say to Sister Mildred, all this must end.

Everything ends sometime, is what her smile says. But she tells me, "The ministry closed the membership in the Shakers ten years ago. The wise heads got together and did a lot of thinking and conferring . . ."

I remind her of a quote in a recent article on the Shakers written by Alan Mast in *Dirigo* magazine. She speaks of Shakerism being a life's work. "Not that it's an easy life . . . I mean, it isn't until you've made it easy. You don't just drift into it and do it well."

Sister Mildred speaks with an air of serenity I admire and envy. "We separate ourselves from the spirit of the world, it's true. But not from the world itself. We welcome people from all races, if they want to be one of us. Negroes, especially from the South. We serve God in the simplest way. We don't need crosses like crutches to lean on. We worship in our everyday living, aiming at perfection in all we do. Perfection is the goal, each in his own craft, in his own style."

What can I tell her?

It's time to go. I say good-by to Sister Mildred and lovely Sister Frances and the others. George must drive to the coast for more pictures. I will drive home, fifteen miles from the Shaker village. I promise to come back soon. I feel a deep affection for these warm, simple people.

Past the Poland Spring House and over the bridge and up the Jackson Road. Live and Let Live. Live and Let Die. No Shaker ever felt economic insecurity. No Shaker ever knew unemployment. No Shaker ever had reason to envy a brother or sister. Down the mountain and round the lake and over the Heath, I'm home. Shakers never raised a hand in violence. They asked only a domain of their own where they could arrange their peaceful useful lives to their liking. And this is how it ends.

THE MAINE MYSTIQUE

It never matters where I stop the car. A gas pump in West Virginia. A motel outside Albuquerque. A scenic turnout near the continental divide. They see the yellow license plate from Maine. Time stops.

"Maine, eh?" A faraway dreamy look. Always that dreamy look.

Maine grabs them. The *idea* of Maine. Reasons vary. It may recall a New England visit years ago. "Got as far as Boston. Never did make it into Maine. Wanted to, real bad. But some day—" Or:

"Maine, eh? I was stationed in Presque Isle [or Portland or Brunswick or Kittery] during the last mess [Vietnam or Korea or World War II]. Ate lobster till it came out of my ears. Listen, if I was to go back—"

Or he's never been to Maine. He read about it in *Field & Stream* and *Sports Afield* and *Reader's Digest.* "Me and the missus has it figured out to get us to Maine, see? We got this little café up for sale. Don't look like much but bein' right here on the highway and all . . . and get us one o' them campers, see—?" That dreamy look. "We'll make it, hear? Me and the missus, some day."

Some day. He's eighty now.

In Arizona they ask about the moose. In Iowa about the corn. In Idaho about the you-know-what. In Georgia they want to know about the birds.

"No quail, mister? Hennery? You heah that? 'S cheah Maine feller jes sayad they ain't no quail shootin wheah he cum fum. Partridge? Never heah tell o' no partridge roun abou'cheah . . ."

A North Michigan deer poacher who pumps gas for a sideline studies the Maine tag and scratches his stubble of jaw. "Vacationland? That mean nobody has got to work?"

They were there once or read about it and nurse the dream. They cling to the dream from childhood, when tales of Maine's virgin forests and clear blue lakes stirred the spirit

of adventure locked in young American hearts. Rockbound coast. Thoreau. Winslow Homer. Evangeline. Logging camps. The river run.

The virgin forests are gone now. Few lakes are clear and blue. Yet the mystique clings. People want Maine to be as they dream it must be or as they remember it. Man seeks freedom from monotony as much as he does freedom from pressure and Maine is the last best thing we have to the natural state. Contentment and fulfillment and serenity, ingredients of that curious American word, happiness.

I realize it when I stop somewhere and see that dreamy look. It needs no words. I know what the man is saying. I drive away gassed-up, oil-checked, blessed by a stranger. The direction I'm going doesn't matter. For me all roads lead to Maine.

The way to Christina's World is well marked with signs. The signs read *Olson House* and point the direction and occasionally give the distance. I feel like a pilgrim en route to a hallowed shrine. And a shrine it may be, judging by the awed and worshipful looks of the visitors I find there.

A first view of the Olson House is startling. It's there, you say to yourself, and it's real. Real enough to make you search the field for Christina half twisted in the tall grass of the field. Illusion vanishes in the presence of a pretty, fresh-faced Maine lady named Laurie Jeanne Starrett. She greets me at the door.

"Visitors come to see the house from places I never even heard of! Gilead, Nebraska! Naples, Florida! Clarkson, Michigan! Carlsbad, California! And from Paris VII, France! Though I've heard of that."

Laurie Jeanne's husband, Wayne, remodeled the Olson House. Laurie Jeanne under Betsy Wyeth's supervision did the interiors and inside painting. "Wonderful people, the Wyeths," she tells me. "Too good to be believed. Andy's a most wonderful man, especially wonderful with children. He's so easy with people, everybody around here tries to protect him. And he deserves it. We live in a fish bowl, you know. We never did before but we do now."

I follow the flow of people through the house. The rooms are carefully restored, and furnished, spare and clean. Furnishings reflect the period and taste of the families that lived there. Original pieces have been used when they were available. Copies are rigorously faithful to their prototypes.

Andrew Wyeth drawings and paintings and some reproductions are hung throughout the house. For me the gems are his preliminary studies of the Olson people. Rough sketches in charcoal and soft pencil, eraser-rubbed, finger-stained, many in black and white wash, the brush strokes overlaid, spot-splashed. The gut sweat of the artist's creative effort laid naked to the eye. The care. Patience. Exasperation. Trial and retrial. The obstinate demand for perfection in each angle of bone, each contour of flesh. Pain is clearly evident in each rubbed line, each erasure, each splash of ink and color.

More than anything here this humble revelation of the artist's ordeal moves me. I will never forget it.

I sign the guest register as I leave. Casco, Maine! "On some days," Laurie Jeanne confides, "we have more than five hundred come through here. On the opening day, that was the sixteenth of June, 1971, we had a nun from Tokyo, Japan!"

Both sky and weatherman that early May morning promised warm sun. It had been an un-speakable winter and this was the first opportunity to thaw the icy marrow in my bones. I chose Popham Beach, loaded typewriter and manuscript and headed east.

From Poland Spring to Topsham the car groped through thick fog. I cursed the weatherman and sure enough the fog burned off on the southerly stretch from Bath. I parked the car, stretched to the sun, climbed the granite tiers of the old fort facing Seguin and the sea. Words from Louis Coxe's *Winter Headland* came to mind.

> *. . . East from the basalt slab*
> *Spain gazes toward you,*
> *Nothing between but drab*
> *Water to ward you:*
> *Flooding beneath your feet*
> *It calls disaster:*
> *Salt on the stiffened cheek*
> *Tells who is master.*

Mouth of the Kennebec. Atlantic salmon once spawned in this river. Here it's 150 miles from its Moosehead Lake source. River god to the Indian, a highway paved with gold for the fur and fish trappers, the lumber barons, the ice cutters. And beyond the mouth, islands named Sugar Loaves, Stage, Pond and Wood. And Seguin with its 1795 lighthouse, tallest on the Maine seacoast.

> *Sequin the lighthouse rock,*
> *Gives vessels entry*
> *Westward to naval dock,*
> *Cradle and gantry*

Fort Popham is a splendid ruin. I climbed gingerly across the huge granite blocks torn loose and flung like playthings by a century of maddened seas. Strangely, the circular stone staircases remain intact. I looked to seaward through the gaping window holes and imagined them as crooked eyes pecked out by sea birds.

Nearby the 1607-8 Popham Colony of English settlers breathed briefly and died. No trace remains. Yet a spell was there that May morning. I felt it in my bones.

I rented a room in one of the gray, weathered cottages that cluster near the point. I set up my typewriter near the window with a view of a narrow patch of the river and went to work.

A week passed quickly. Days of rewriting, nights of quiet except for the wind and sea. And always the gut loneliness of the writer with his thoughts. My story dealt with men at sea in ships of war. When a work goes well and if the writer is lucky, he moves into the world of his story. So that what he is writing, the made-up characters and events, become real to him and he lives and breathes as a flesh-and-blood witness to his imagined scene.

In just such a state I found myself deep into the emotions of weary men in an obsolete warship in Aleutian waters under the worst possible conditions of weather and morale. As I wrote I smelled the icy sea air and the paint and steel and gunsmoke smells. I heard the orders and commands of officers and the raw talk of seamen. I felt the tension of imminent violence at sea. The ship's motion, the throb of turbines—

The throb of turbines seemed closer than before. A ship's squawk box crackled to life. I heard the shrill bleat of a bosun's pipe. My fingers fell from the typewriter. This was *not* in the script.

I shut my eyes. Had I been banging away at the machine too long? Deranged by my own intense visions? The bosun's pipe came shrill and clear. I opened my eyes.

Not five hundred yards from my window, a navy warship midstream in the Kennebec headed for the open sea, signal flags flapping. Navy and civilian personnel swarmed over her decks. I slumped with relief.

She was a spanking new destroyer making a trial run from the shipyard upstream at Bath where she had been built. I watched her steam by, a lovely sight to a sometime sailor. I stood and saluted.

It was my muse I saluted, really. She had outdone herself. When I sat again and faced the page of typing, the words flowed like honey.

That was then. Popham's changed some. A state park draws thousands each summer. Cottage developments have changed much of the natural look of the area. Yet the old spell of the ancient day is still there. In a private field nearby a stone bears runic markings believed by some to have been made by Norse seamen early in the eleventh century. Others less romantic think it the markings of somebody's grandfather's plow.

Man comes and man goes, but Louis Coxe is right. The sea is master.

JOURNAL NOTE: Except for TV, electricity and inside plumbing, country people in Maine choose to live pretty much in the style of their forebears. The antiques in their homes are there because they belonged to a Revolutionary or Civil War grandparent, not because they caught someone's eye in a U.S. 1 antique shop.

I knew a family in Monmouth, poor as church mice, who ate their meals for years off the same chipped, purple-bordered dishes. It wasn't until the place burned to the ground and we were salvaging a few charred pieces that any of us knew it was old and rare Wedgwood earthenware, brought over from England by their forebears.

She was built in 1964, steel-hulled, 65 feet from stem to stern and certified for sea travel up to fifty miles offshore. A rugged craft with a tender name. They call her God's Tugboat. She's *Sunbeam IV*, sixth in a succession of Mission vessels. The work began with a single missionary in a little sloop, the *Hope*, whose efforts the winter of 1905–06 indicated both the potential for service and the need for a better ship. The motor launch *Morning Star* was given in 1907. In 1912, the first *Sunbeam* was built especially for the work, replaced in 1926 by *Sunbeam II* and in 1939 by *Sunbeam III*.

The Mission is the everyday name of the Maine Sea Coast Missionary Society. Its founders stated in part that "the purpose of the Society is to undertake religious and benevolent work in the neglected communities and among the isolated families along the coast and on the islands of Maine." Since that time the scope of endeavors has widened, meaning more things to many more people. A scholarship for a deserving high school student who otherwise could not afford college. Companionship to shut-ins. Talking books for the blind. Spiritual comfort to the bereaved.

Needs change with the times. The Mission never quits, constantly facing each new challenge with understanding, compassion and action. The dedication of its staff, which is scattered widely over the coastal communities and islands, is reflected in these sample reports made during the harsh winter of 1970–71:

DEC. 21 Still very cold but 16 adults and children piled into three cars and went caroling at two nursing homes and for several shut-ins scattered over a 20-mile area. I got some sort of chill and didn't leave the house again until Jan. 2.

DEC. 24 High winds and snow. Looks like a blizzard in the making. By late afternoon, all roads were clogged. Did not cancel 11 P.M. service but no one came.

DEC. 24 This morning I took the talking machine book to Roy, some cookies to Roland and a book to Clara. In the afternoon, some folks came for a snowshoe trek on the trails. . . . the storm began to worsen so I took a short cut and met them at the entrance. By the time we had served hot chocolate and seen them headed home, the storm was such that I called the deacons of the two churches that were planning a combined Christmas Eve service. All agreed. Cancel!

DEC. 27 Dug path to church at 6 A.M. Wind blowing hard. Did not cancel service and five people came.

DEC. 27 Church was called off. The snow plow broke down and it wasn't until 2 P.M. that we were able to get out, through the use of a front-end loader . . .

DEC. 30 Still digging. Now on the lower area of the roofs. Ice dams have formed and water is streaming into the pantry.

The parish takes in 250 miles of seacoast and the outlying islands. Ashore, the work is carried on in jeeps, trucks, cars and on foot. But to a Coastguardsman in a lonely lighthouse on some forsaken jut of rock, or to a handful of the island fishermen's children, it's the sound of her whistle and the sight of God's Tugboat breaking through the fog and ice floes in black weather that has spiritual significance, as though the Lord Himself reached out to touch their hands.

Over the years, God's Tugboats have carried, in addition to the Good Word, mail, people and anything else from hogsheads for salt fish to jeeps. Transportation for island burials is provided as needed. At Matinicus, twenty miles southeast of Rockland, there were five in the period from June 1969, to May 1970. Islanders are not ungrateful. A blanket made from the wool of sheep raised on Matinicus served for twenty-five years aboard *Sunbeam III*. It's one of hundreds of gifts the Mission has received.

Why does anyone bother? Isn't God dead?

The Reverend Neal D. Bousfield, Mission Superintendent 1938–72, knows why. He writes, "Our roots are deep in the Maine coast, and its people continue to look to us as a reliable bulwark against the shifting sands of change. We are confident that the young people who are being helped with Mission scholarships will continue to put their education to good use. One of our island boys is going to get his master's degree before going into a missionary field. Others are preparing for teaching and nursing. These young people are not unaware of the restlessness about them but most of them have strong religious roots and we have no doubt that it is they and their kind who will be among the leaders of to-morrow."

JOURNAL NOTE: I'm on the upstairs porch of Winslow Homer's studio at Prout's Neck, facing the sea. It isn't often one can have a national historic landmark all to one's self and a hallowed view of the sea in absolute solitude. A section of the railing blew away in last week's storm and lays half buried in stiff winter grass across a crooked path lost in a snarl of juniper. To seaward South Stratton and Bluff Islands sprawl over the metallic sea and in distant mist to the south a tower stands over Biddeford Pool.

The clapboards of this summer studio are green and the trim white and if the paint is peeling, I remind myself that's not what matters here. Yellow lichen thrives in the seams of a graceful chimney. The juniper trunks are twisted like the rare Torrey pines of California. Did Homer's own hands plant them here?

Inside in the central room his easel stands, a naked brown geometry draped with a pair of ladies' kid gloves, arm-length and stiff with age. Whose? If I touch them will they crumble to dust? I have a feeling at once the action has stopped, the way it does in TV segments, to hold you in your seat until the commercials run. Freeze-dried, I think, to come alive again when tourists troop through here come summer.

The walls of all the rooms are hung with prints of Homer paintings; too small, too faded; some of them valuable, I judge, but not many. Trout nets, delicate deer skulls, old wooden noisemakers (we used to call them "groggers"), a moose rack, countless swords and daggers. Old books on several shelves, revealing no pattern of thought or taste; the only one to catch my eye: *The Present State of Hayti* by James Franklin, inscribed on the flyleaf, C. S. Homer, London 1857.

A summer cottage is at its dreariest in March. I leave and lock up. A strong steady wind rustles the juniper and puckerbrush, and down below the studio, waves are writhing over the rocks. A lone gull sweeps overhead. He painted gulls so well. The sound of the sea is constant, paced by a hollow clanking of a buoy bell in the small bay.

176

WHAT THE EARTH HOLDS

Deer Isle is sheer joy. A tatter of green-fringed woodland, down and heath, granite-rooted to the sea. Hardy sailors, boat builders and fishermen shared its unspoiled beauty for over two hundred years, shut off from the despoiling world except for a ferry from the mainland carrying a few venturesome artists and summer folk.

Now the drive south in springtime crosses Eggemoggin Reach by minibridge and a stone causeway. In the village called Sunshine at the island's eastern tip, the Haystack Mountain School of Crafts provides a summer *atelier* for artists and craftsmen from all over the world. At Les Chalets Français in Mountainville, nice girls are taught proper French and the rudiments of outdoor Maine living. The views of Penobscot Bay and the outer islands from the village called Sunset are unsurpassed anywhere along the Maine coast.

I'm tempted to linger but I'm going to Stonington. I choose a road that leads me past trim, still-shut clapboard summer places. The steel blue face of Southeast Harbor reveals itself from time to time between dense stands of pine, fir and spruce. A scenic peekaboo. It should cheer me. Instead, I'm saddened by the drained carcasses of beer cans still in their plastic six-pack collars glinting in the gully, and chrome strips on a foundered chassis of rust in a dooryard choked with dead weeds.

But the fiddleheads are sprouting and Stonington is a friendly place. Strangers nod as I cruise slowly down Main Street at the harbor's edge. Their faces are cheerful. Some say Hi as though we're old friends or neighbors. I feel welcome in Stonington.

Wherever I look I see slabs of rough granite. Square-cut, oblong, cubed, a ton to ten tons each, awesome as Fort Knox. They line walks, border well-kept gardens, mark the seawalls facing the bay. Sills, foundations, bulkheads, wharves, each stone positioned, you'd think, as lightly as children's blocks. All from the Stonington earth. Here to stay long after man is gone.

The way it was, every Stonington man who didn't follow the sea worked the "kwurries." Deer Isle quarries provided the pink granite for the Washington Monument, the Kennedy Memorials, Rockefeller Center, the Triborough Bridge, the Cathedral of St. John the Divine.

The stonecutters and quarrymen of this slumberous village belong to a proud guild of craftsmen. They pass their skills, father to son, in a calling as ancient as the days of hand-chisels and oxen, but I actually know little more than that about quarrying. I pay a visit to the town office and Arnold "Doc" Brown, the town manager, provides a few facts.

Granite is abundant the world over. It is one of the densest of stones, weighting 170 pounds per cubic feet. Its name originally meant any coarse crystalline igneous rock. It retains that popular meaning today, though scientists now designate such rocks as *phanerites* and limit the word granite to stone composed wholly of quartz and feldspar combined with small amounts of mica and other minerals. It is the reddish feldspar content that gives the coveted pink color to Deer Isle granite. The 3,500-year-old Egyptian obelisk of Heliopolis called "Cleopatra's Needle" which now stands in New York's Central Park is of just such granite as Deer Isle's.

In its natural state, granite is laid up in "onionskin" strata and quarried sheet by sheet, a seam between each layer. In the old days, the quarrymen drilled with black powder. Now they burn with oxygen, fuel oil and compressed air. The huge sheet or block first freed is prime granite called the saw block. The quarrymen heft it to the gang saws, a series of iron blades that, under the skilled hands of the stonecutters, split the saw block into slabs.

Stonecutters are the highly skilled specialists of the quarry, an elite group, the highest paid of the working crews. They have studied the character of granite since childhood, listening to and watching their fathers and grandfathers, who keep to themselves the secret lore of grain and color, channel and joint, seam and wedge.

It was a prosperous industry until the introduction of macadam and concrete stole away the paving block and building stone business from the granite men. The Depression of the thirties paralyzed the industry. The postwar building boom brought a heartening revival but not enough to keep the granite interests in the black.

As recently as 1958 twelve quarries were working full blast in the Deer Isle area. Most of them are shut down now. Nobody seems quite sure about reopening the quarries. Perhaps half the town is on welfare. Many cutters and derrickmen and administrative office help have turned to lobstering for a livelihood. ". . . Until the kwurries opens up again," they say. But the future looks dim.

Perhaps it's just as well. For a man who works the quarries, good times or bad, is likely to end up a terminal case. Silicosis. Stone dust inhaled lines his lungs and stays there. To work is to die and not to work is to starve. Even when he wins he loses.

I listen in on all this at about ten in the morning round the back table of the School Street Restaurant. Folks keep dropping in. Linnie Eckles keeps the coffee cups full and the fresh doughnuts coming. Ruth and Lionel Barbour own and run the lunchroom. Ruth is a formidable cook who measures a full two ounces of clear chunky lobster meat into her lobster rolls. They've been around Stonington most of their lives. Ruth's father, Arthur Carter, and Lionel's father, William, both died the same year. 1942. Silicosis.

Merrill Allen drops by. He's a town selectman, young, earnest, a maverick. Right now the town's caught up in a high school hassle. Everybody agrees the area needs a consolidated school but they can't get together on where to build it. Between the mainland and the surrounding islands they count 800 registered voters. Coffee splashes. Doughnuts get dunked. The talk is sharp, heated, never hostile. No decision this round but it's clear that feelings run deep.

Buster Sawyer, quarryman, switched to lobstering. Had to, he says. Lungs. Ten years ago he was getting forty cents a pound for his lobsters, ". . . and a man could live good on that." Now lobsters are scarce and the price is out of sight. "I'd go back to the kwurries in a minute, was they workin'."

Guy Barbour joins in. He quit the quarries because he contracted TB. I look at him. Bone thin. He reads my thoughts. "Used to weigh one-seventy," he says, proud. "Went down to one-twelve." His eyes brighten. He's recalling what it was like in Stonington's heyday. Quarrymen and stonecutters used to assemble on Main Street in the evenings after work and supper, spruced up and clean, full of a hard day's work and fish chowder. They'd stand around smoking, exchanging the gossip of the day. Kids like Buster would hang around goggle-eyed and listen. These were the big men of the boats and quarries spinning their yarns about fish and stone.

Bob McGuffie sits with the School Street regulars, a bit aloof like a courtroom judge. He's seen the outside world. He's been as far west as St. Cloud, Wisconsin, working the quarries. Always working the quarries. It wasn't until fifteen years ago, Bob says, that the state finally got around to giving quarry workers free X rays at regular intervals. "Now a feller can know how much stone dust has got to him, not that it makes a difference when he's bringin' home a full week's pay."

McGuffie recalls a time in a quarry when he had a fifteen-foot sheet of granite weighing eight tons over his head. The derrickman working the rig lost control and the stone plunged downward. It just missed him.

He shakes his head. "One way or t'other, there ain't much comfort in knowin' you're going to end up under a polished slab of the same damn stuff that robbed you of the best years of your life."

The water in my well comes bubbling and racing out of the house taps chill and clear. I come into the kitchen from the garden or orchard hot and thirsty; I run the water a few seconds and fill a big tumbler and knock it back. It courses through me cold and wet and I tell myself no liquid in the time of man, ambrosia or nectar or whatever, can be as sweetly refreshing as this water from my well. And I fill the tumbler and knock it back again.

Wells are at least as old as Rebekah. In Maine, we have three kinds of wells: dug, driven and drilled. Dug wells are the real old-timers. The farmer would go out back and dig himself a big round hole and keep digging until he struck water. He'd let it settle overnight; then he'd fill the bottom with rocks and white beach sand to keep the mud out of it.

He'd line the hole with a dry wall of rocks, building it to three feet or so above the ground to keep out leaves and surface water. All it took after that was a wooden reel with a handle and enough rope and a wooden bucket and he was in business.

Pumps came along, first hand-made of wood; then cast iron. A pipe was run almost to the bottom of the well and the pump was threaded to the top and primed with a bucket or two of water. The first pipes were made of lead, then galvanized iron, then copper, brass and now plastic. Dug wells are still in use, but the water supply they yield no longer meets the needs of homes with inside plumbing, automatic washing machines, dishwashers and such.

Driven wells are just that—sections of pipe driven, by pounding, into the ground. Inch-and-a-half or two-inch pipe is attached to a bronze well point, a reasonably sharp, finely screened and tapered tip that probes downward with each pounding. Five-foot lengths of pipe are threaded to the top until water is struck, seeping into the well point below. Sometimes the pipe will strike rock first. She may go by; if she won't, the pipe is pulled out and set over and driven again. All that shows above ground, with a driven well, is the end of the pipe and the pump.

Drilled wells are most common these days in the country. Well drilling is big business today, requiring huge rigs on wheels to haul the power-driven rotary machines to get down to where the water is supposed to be. Ten years ago it was a kind of loosely run operation. Today's dues-paying well driller belongs to the National Water Well Association (which held its annual convention in Las Vegas this past year), and all sorts of scientific and technical information is passed around.

A man having a well drilled can never know in advance what it's going to cost him. Well drillers charge seven dollars a foot plus two-fifty for each foot of well casing. An 8¾″ drill goes in first, through loam, gravel, stones, hardpan, (all of which is called "overburden"), until it hits solid ledge. It drives on through the ledge for at least five feet and is withdrawn. The hole is air-blown clean of foreign matter and obstructions and a six-inch black steel casing is then inserted to seal out the surface water. A jackhammer, fitting inside the casing, goes the rest of the way until a good vein of water is struck.

The modern equipment used today can drill as deep as five hundred feet. It can be the house owner's nightmare. At a hundred feet with no water, he begins to worry. At two hundred, he knows he'll be drinking plain water at imported scotch prices. By the time the drill's down to three hundred feet with no more than a dribble to show for it, he's probably considering a change of location. If he hasn't already shot himself.

To make sure they'll find water, some people call in a dowser. For twenty-five dollars, a dowser will walk over your land with a forked stick, a coat hanger, a piece of copper wire or some gizmo of his own invention, and tell you where to dig for water. He's usually right, but there's no telling how much water there is or how long it will last. Kenneth Roberts of Kennebunkport was a great believer in dowsing.

I'm a great believer in my well. It's never run dry.

PEOPLE AND PLACES . . .

Do not leave Stonington without a visit to Freedman's century-old dry goods store. Drive out West Main Street hard by the Opera House (a startling landmark displaying nothing more than architectural vulgarity and double feature movies) and look for the store-front sign, S. Freedman & Co. on the left. No parking problems here. The trade is slow and not always steady.

Henry Freedman is a cheerful optimist. He's turned sixty and looks ten years younger. He was born in Stonington, lived in Stonington all of his life. His father, Simon, a native of Minsk, came to Stonington as a peddler from New York. He found an active market for his wares, and clean fresh air, and settled permanently. Henry's older brother, Israel, 73, runs the store with him.

Henry is a bachelor. He lives in the apartment over the store, where he was born. He is pink-cheeked, slight, Dickensian. His smile is disarming, his business disposition shyly Yankee. In a few minutes he has much of my life story and I have bought and paid for a T-shirt and shorts I really don't need.

He settles himself comfortably against a thick cylinder of rolled shiny linoleum (9' x 12', $5.99). He's met writers before, he says. "Fellow with a beard came in here a few years ago. Had a little dog and he wanted to know was it all right to bring the dog in. Polite as could be. So I told him, sure, bring the dog in. And he did. A lady was in here shopping and she grabs my arm and she says do I know who that is and I didn't and she tells me it was John Steinbeck."

"Traveling with Charley," I say.

"How should I know who was with him?" His blue eyes are innocent. "He bought a few nice things and he paid cash." Henry smiles. "You ever hear of an artist, John Marin? John Marin used to come in here a lot. Used to sit in that chair right over there." I looked at the worn blessed chair. "Not only artists and writers. Nelson Rockefeller, right off his boat. A big spender."

I admire and envy serene Henry Freedman who has brushed sleeves with greatness and sold a few pairs of socks and perhaps a wool cap in the bargain. Henry Freedman, native of Stonington, Maine, who has lived nowhere else all of his life.

"Tell me, Henry, why you've always stayed in Stonington."

"It's a living." He points a bony finger at a few wire hangers where three blue denim work jackets hang disconsolately from the overhead. "Can you use a good denim jacket? A real bargain, mister. A hundred per cent wool-lined."

I resist the denim jacket. His eyes are measuring me for a pair of corduroy slacks. "Tell me, Henry, how you managed to stay unmarried all these years. An attractive man like you."

"You know what they say, don't you?"

"What do they say?"

"Marriage isn't a word. It's a sentence."

"And living alone, do you keep a kosher house?"

He nods. "And I go to Boston for the high holidays."

I gather up my purchases and shake Henry's hand. "I like your store, Henry. It's simple and unpretentious. It has style, a certain *Je ne sais pas de quoi.*"

"I get plenty of French customers, too. From Canada."

"I also admire you for living in the place where you were born. You're as much a part of Stonington as its granite."

"Thank you."

"But you disappoint me, Henry."

He looks alarmed. "What disappoints you?"

"I point to the doorway. "No *mezuzah,* Henry."

"Not there, no." His smile is relieved, beatific. "But you should see upstairs. There I have three *mezuzahs.*"

Sometimes when the day-to-day going gets heavy, I climb into the car and drive two hundred miles to Machias to observe the George Thurston family. George teaches American history. His wife Ruth is a librarian. They live with their six children in a big old-fashioned house with high ceilings and a gentle slope of tillable land down to the Machias River. I just go and sit there and watch them. It relaxes me. George's and Ruth's people have lived in Down East Maine a long time. George went to Bowdoin College, quit a good university job in Pennsylvania after the war to return to Maine where he felt he was needed. They lived in Sorrento and Sullivan while George taught school and the family grew. Now they're settled in Machias and the kids are growing up. The oldest girl (there are five) is away at the University of Maine at Orono. Tommy is a rugged young man, starting college now, athlete, worm-digger and retired collector of rare bottles. The children are bright, witty, articulate, obedient. They do as they're told. Cheerfully. That's what attracts me, what I find so fascinating. Cheerful obedience.

Some might call George an enlightened despot. He's enlightened all right, and firm, but he's no despot. He believes that to keep a household of eight on the move, somebody has to be in charge. It's the only practical way to keep a large family from stepping all over themselves.

The best time to do family-watching at George's and Ruth's commune is early morning. There's one bathroom. The schedule is rigid—twelve minutes per person, starting at 6:30 A.M. I watch in stunned disbelief as the morning ritual unfolds. Everyone knows his job. They move about with the quiet certainty of a trained ballet group, a drill team, a surgeon's staff in the operating room. Teeth are being brushed, porridge is cooking, lunches are packing, beds are being made. Conversation is normal (bright). There is no anger, no sign of mutiny.

Breakfast is served, dishes are washed and stacked. There is a last-minute scurrying for books, lunches, clothing; final instructions and admonitions and they're off—to school, to job, dead on schedule. I sit and marvel at the wonder of it and shakily pour a second cup of coffee.

What is truly remarkable about the Thurstons is the absence of anger. The day is launched in an atmosphere of congenial banter and cheerful bickering. No voice is raised. None of the children needs prodding. They may not agree with George's or Ruth's dicta but none would consider for a moment not doing what he's told. It isn't that George cannot raise his voice. I've heard it, during the years we worked together in a Maine summer camp. George was the head counselor. No PA system was needed. George's bellowing took care of that and the probable loudspeaker needs of the girls' camp across the lake.

Watching the Thurstons start a day restores my faith in the old-fashioned American tradition of home. The sharing of chores. The evening meal followed by studies, relaxation and good talk. Other families in America must run their lives like this, but I wonder how many there are, and if there are as many as there were a year ago. Five years ago. Too many families these days break up before their time. Too many disintegrate for social, economic or emotional reasons. For selfish reasons. Too many young people take to the road and never return. There is nothing to return to. There never was.

Psychologists and sociologists know the answers, I guess. I just wanted to say how good it makes me feel, Thurston-watching, the whole gang pulling together, each pulling his own weight. I guess that's what pulls me there, and props my sagging faith in the American family.

You reach the Roosevelt family's summer cottage on Campobello Island by crossing the International Bridge at Lubec. The cottage is now part of a 2,600-acre international park. A pretty young lady, Mrs. Vera Calder at the new Reception Centre informed me her mother had worked for the Roosevelt family. That's how I came to meet Mrs. Linnea Calder, receptionist at Roosevelt Campobello International Park.

When she was a small child, Mrs. Calder's father was a caretaker on the estate. He died when she was six and her mother started working for the Roosevelts. Her mother was Swedish, Mrs. Calder says, and came to Campobello with the Hubbard family, who had the house next door to the Roosevelts.

"She started in as a laundress," Mrs. Calder recalls, "and worked for them for over forty years. She became their housekeeper during that time. After the President's death she went to New York. She was sort of Mrs. Roosevelt's housekeeper-companion."

"Were you here when the President came down with polio?"

"That was in 1921. I was here, yes, but I remember it only because of hearing about it afterwards."

Mrs. Calder was born on Campobello and went to school here. She doesn't think life on the island has changed very much in that time. "I can remember the first car on Campobello and the first radio and all of those things. But it still looks pretty much the same. We had twenty-five or thirty summer families in this section of the island, but the Roosevelts were the only ones who became really famous."

"Did you know FDR's mother?"

"Yes. Very well. She was a great lady. She was married to a man who was a lot older than she was and Franklin was her only child and I think she had a strong influence on him. Many people find fault with her, but she must have been all right or he wouldn't have made out as good as he did."

"Did you ever have a chance to talk with the President?"

"Oh, yes. I worked at the Roosevelt cottage in 1933, when he was here. He was friendly, very friendly. They were a wonderful family to work for. All of them."

"Did you have any favorites among the five children?"

"Well, I think probably Franklin, Jr., is my favorite. And I liked Elliott. James and Anna were older. Johnny was much younger. There were some who did not like Elliott or did not approve of him at times but he was O.K. and I liked him very much."

Driving out to Beal's Island in late July (where, I'm told, there are more days of fog than clear), George came across Ralph Brown in Jonesport shelling peas, and took some pictures. I came by a week later. Peas were still flourishing in the garden. I found Ralph inside fixing himself a cup of coffee. I joined him. Ralph's an easy talker.

"George told me you're a teacher. What grades?"

"Six and seven. In Cherryfield, just back up the road. Not regular, though. Last winter I was working in the Thomaston cement plant and I got laid off right after New Year's. Then this opening occurred over there to Cherryfield. I'm getting a lot less money than I would in construction but it's a lot easier. I suppose the end result of the whole thing is, I'm making use of some of the education I had."

"This is boatbuilding country. Did you ever work on boats?"

"You have to be a real craftsman for that. The kind of work I do is rough. I have a friend over on Beal's Island who's a boatbuilder. A great practical joker. One day I went in and they use an adz to shape the keel, an oak keel, and this is six inches thick. That piece of wood is worth a lot of money. He's got this adz and is swinging away like someone playing golf. I said to him, 'What happens if you cut that a little too deep?' And he hands me the adz. 'Here,' he says, 'Take it and try it.' He was actually willing for me to actually go to work with that thing and he has that piece of wood there that must have cost him a hundred dollars or so and he has spent several days shaping it out."

Ralph's boy Floyd joins us. He's an eighth grader. I ask him if he plans to leave Maine when he grows up, like so many young people do.

"I like it right where I am," says Floyd.

"Would you consider being a lobster fisherman?"

"I'm not sure."

"What about building boats?"

"I don't think I want to be a boatbuilder."

"But you want to do something that's part of Maine, don't you?"

"Yes." As though no other thought ever entered his mind.

His father says, "These vocational schools they have under way now are real desirable. If I had to go back and start all over again, that's where I'd have been. Outside, though. I got to have fresh air and physical exertion. That's the nature of me."

Ralph suggests I take a look around Beal's Island. "Just drive around," he says. "You'll see boats sitting in back yards. You'll see 'em where you'd think it's impossible, where there's no way to get that thing to the water. They just set up on molds, what they call them, and start in and they'll work on it right through the winter, right outside. They'll put up a canopy here and there when they need to. They don't need any fancy place to work. Or fancy tools, either. It's by instinct they build. Just a natural flair. I couldn't build a boat without it being lopsided. They do it by eye. The Jonesport model, that was the pattern for most of the lobster boats on the coast."

"Do they build any fiber glass here?"

"Not that I know of."

I shop in the town of Norway, sixteen miles from my dooryard. The pace is easy and there's always time to drop in at the Weary Club and see what the boys are up to.

I find them up to the usual. George Ames and Perley Merrill, for example. They're reading. Ralph Stone's in a back corner. He's thinking. George is seventy-six; Perley's seventy-two; Ralph's a youngster of fifty-nine. I sit down and light up and lean back. All I hear is the ticking of the big Ansonia wall clock.

The Weary Club occupies a one-story modified Greek Revival building on Norway's main street; it has white clapboards, green shutters and a flagpole. The club was started by Fred Sanborn, former publisher of the Norway *Adviser-Democrat*, who came from Meredith, New Hampshire, fifty years ago. It began as a whittling club, a kind of sanctuary for the men in town to sit around and chew the fat and, of course, whittle. Whittle they did. The floor would be covered inches deep with shavings. Cribbage came along, and checkers and card games. Gambling and drinking are still forbidden, as are females, either transient or resident.

Perley used to drive the bus between Norway and Paris (a matter of a few miles in Maine). It was an old Chevvy seating twenty. Perley's big moment came when he carried the jurors back and forth to the courthouse during the 1938 Littlefield murder trial.

George's family were early settlers of Norway, grinding the first grist, building the first dam on Norway Lake and sawing the first lumber. George was a car mechanic at twelve, working on one-lung Reos and Cadillacs and a two-cylinder Maxwell in Frank Beard's garage. "Nothing much to learn about a car in those days," he recalls, "they were that simple." He stayed with cars for thirty-five years until he retired.

Ralph Stone retired two years ago. It broke my heart. Ralph bakes the best custard pie known to man. He learned to cook in a Brown Company lumber camp in Grafton, Maine. About half the lumberjacks were Yankees; the rest were Frenchmen, Poles, Finns and Swedes. Ralph went through a barrel of flour a day, baking bread and biscuits, cakes and pies for the crew.

I first tasted Ralph's custard pie twenty years ago in the Bar-Jo Café. It's a fancier place now, with tablecloths and a wine and cocktail list. Ralph tells me his wife bakes the custard pies now, using the same recipe, and swears you can't tell the difference. For each pie, he uses eight fresh eggs, pure vanilla, fresh milk, sugar and nutmeg. No shortening, no cornstarch. The pies are baked the night before and refrigerated so they stand firm in the morning, with no water on the bottom and no soggy crust. "The water," Ralph confides, "means the pie baked too long."

I went down to Kennebunk to talk to Sandy Brook about the way things are in his end of seacoast Maine. A lot of people in southern Maine don't get along too well with Sandy. He speaks a hard truth. It isn't only the way he speaks that irritates them. It's what he publishes in his newspaper, the York County *Coast Star*. About pollution and politics and the troubles of tourism.

They write in with a full head of steam. They tell Sandy to get the hell out if he doesn't like Maine. But Sandy Brook loves Maine. That's why he speaks and writes as he does.

"One of the charms of Maine is that it's poor. I'd rather see a run-down fisherman's shack along the coast than a new motel. I went down to Barrington, Rhode Island, a while ago. [Barrington's a place that feeds Providence with people like professors at Brown University.] The place has the sterility of wealth. You can ride for miles and see nothing but manicured lawns and clipped hedges. There isn't a house that needs a coat of paint. The new cars are polished hard. Beyond Barrington you come out on a dilapidated riverfront with old brick factories and warehouses. The docks are falling into the water. The old brick is weathered. You get a sudden lift—you're back in a working community.

"You can't imagine an artist going into Barrington and setting up his easel in front of one of those manicured hundred-thousand-dollar homes. You'll find him sitting across the harbor painting this row of run-down factory buildings and all the dilapidation. It's picturesque, kind of toney . . ."

I suggest that Eastport is like that. A disaster area to everybody except the people who live there.

Sandy shakes his head. "I don't like to see Eastport's kind of decay. That's jobless poverty and people with no transportable skills and roots too deep to move. But there has to be an alternative to a refinery. It's too bad when people have to move out to find jobs, forced to leave the old places they grew up in. But to save a handful from welfare, you don't wreck a coast."

"That's progress, isn't it? Tearing up the old to make way for the new."

"Depends on where it's happening. If it's building up the local downtown main street, trying to make it attractive for shoppers, giving the people who live there a chance to spend their money at home, that's one thing. But here it's tourist-oriented. Ninety per cent of the money the chambers of commerce spend is on brochures to lure tourists here to litter the place. And every morning, starting about seven o'clock all year round, the wide loads roll up Route 1 like old elephants. Mobile homes. The escort cars say WIDE LOAD FOLLOWING and WIDE LOAD AHEAD, and you don't know where they're going. You begin to think there must be some wide load graveyard up yonder.

"I hate these package homes. Everybody says, 'Would you rather have a tar paper shack?' I would. Tar paper shacks don't bother me any more than the dilapidated buildings across the river. The shacks belong to people who originated here. They're building little shacks for their families. They're going out in the woods to cut pulpwood. Eventually they'll put clapboards on the place and raise their kids as their Maine ancestors did. Fine."

Thomaston's main street on U.S. 1 is a busy place in summer when the tourists stop off at the prison store to buy gifts and gadgets and good solid furniture made by the inmates. It was a trading post in 1630 and became incorporated in 1777.

Times have changed since 1840, when two Thomaston sea captains were among the seven millionaires of record in the United States. Fine houses still stand, though the prosperity of a century ago has vanished. Down one of Thomaston's handsome tree-shaded side streets I find Harry Stump at work in the dooryard of his home, an imposing Greek Revival mansion needing little more than paint and a post or two to restore its original beauty. It's known as the Walsh home. Walshes once owned shipyards here. The Stumps have lived in it for two years.

Harry is a sculptor in welded steel. Steel has meaning for Harry Stump. He was a Dutch Resistance fighter at sixteen and spent a few years behind bars and steel fences in the Gestapo prison camp in Maastricht.

He's reluctant to talk about it and very busy welding. He works feverishly, fitting fiber glass and stained glass into twisted forms of junk metal. His figures emerge as gracefully as butterflies and slender as chance. Many of them are madonnas. The technique is known as found art. Harry calls it "Drawings in Space."

It's a nice Sunday afternoon. People drive by, slow down, stop. Some come over to watch Harry work and to inspect the finished pieces in the barn which is full of Harry Stump originals.

Harry's wife Susie discreetly handles visitors and chores and any diversions that might annoy Harry while he works. She believes in him and that's good. Harry's art is good enough to believe in. If he sells enough sculpture, Susie confides, he won't have to go back to tending bar in Thomaston.

JOURNAL NOTE: One of the obscure but immensely satisfying rewards of Maine living is to listen to Joe Green on WBZ Radio in Boston and not be there. WBZ is received loud and clear in most of Maine. Joe Green delivers the rush hour traffic reports from a helicopter (painted green, of course), several times a day.

His style is pure frenzy mixed with the ear-shattering staccato of a machine gun. Green's overview of the overload in the Sumner Tunnel or along Storrow Drive or on the Mystic River Bridge carries a chill foreboding of imminent disaster. At any moment you expect absolute chaos—as though all drivers and their vehicles in a communal agony of frustration will throw caution to the winds and meet head on, side on, tail on, crashing and exploding in all directions, showering bits and pieces of flesh, bone, plastic and steel over half of Boston.

The best time to hear Joe, of course, is when you're driving north on the empty Maine Turnpike. Or into the village to pick up the mail. Or settled down by the blazing hearth with a cup of tea laced with Yankee rum and nothing else around to compete with Joe's jabbering but the cry of a passing loon.

. . . AND HOW
THE WEATHER WAS

Like wood and stone, Maine people are shaped by the elements. A brutal winter bends a man. Frost fastens him in place. In the warmth of late spring he opens the earth, trickling a dark moist handful through his grateful fingers. Moist crumbling sweet-smelling earth breathing life in the sun. A handful of life itself.

The winters erode Maine people. Locked between sea and snow, life can be chancy. Some never make it to spring. On my hill at the side of the road an old granite vault hollowed out of the soil beneath a graveyard bears testimony to the hard life. Here the winter dead rest in deep freeze until the earth above relents enough for decent burial.

Most Maine winters are frozen hell. The summertime and autumn can be paradise. And there is a purgatory of sorts, somewhere between winter and springtime. A time of despair and stone-cold marrow, when the most cheerful and reverent of people swear at their loved ones and wish they were dead.

Call it the season of despond. For a month to as much as eight weeks it puts the stout-hearted Maine spirit to its severest test. Snow loads crush roof timbers. Melting ice seeps under shingles, soaks ceiling plaster, dribbles on bedsheets and floods floors. Power fails. Roads turn to glass. Car batteries whimper and die.

The mind bumbles. Reason flounders. Strong men waver and wilt. Sound-minded women grow giddy or testy and weep often. Only children in their innocence seem untouched and thrive.

Some call it cabin fever. The symptoms are varied — delusion, lethargy, depression, insomnia, hallucination, drunkenness, adultery. In Canada's northwest territory it's known as northern hysteria, but it's the same thing.

The Maine winter of 1970–71 was one of the worst in history. Deep snow drifts shut off people from their world for weeks on end. Dean Rhodes of the Bangor *News* bureau in Presque Isle got out and around that winter and talked to a mixed bag of County people in an effort to understand this mysterious winter malady. He found an eighty-two-year-old

204

semi-retired woods guide bent over his bowl of chicken gizzard stew. The old man had no appetite. The worsening winter had got to him and all he could do was brood sentimentally over his mother and father, long dead. "I don't know what else to do," he lamented, "once I get to thinking."

A Presque Isle man caught hell from his wife because he had neglected to re-wrap the cheese properly. Her venom and his distemper drove him from the house. He was sitting in his office alone, sulking, wishing he had some way to get to the Virgin Islands for a while.

One sturdy old-timer who makes canoe poles and ax handles didn't quite know what had happened to him. "Never made an ax handle. Never filed a saw. Didn't do nothin' all winter," he muttered. "Sat an' watched the cars go by. M'house was buried so deep, had to lower the snowbank to see the road. Felt kinda lonesome-like, y'know?"

Rhodes consulted hospital officials. They all agreed the problem ("It's more a problem than an illness") could be serious for those affected by it. "You're no longer stimulated," a mental health clinic director explained. "You see the same faces and snowbanks for four or five months. You know exactly what you're going to be doing next Wednesday at eight-fifteen. With nothing to do, your functioning falls off so that you and others around you aren't satisfied with it."

A surgeon pointed out that work is man's therapy. He admitted that in his own case he found lack of winter activity demoralizing. The hardest hit by cabin fever are the elderly and retired, those without financial or imaginative resources; those unable to get away for a visit or a trip elsewhere; those unable to entertain themselves at home.

It doesn't seem to bother Dennis Pelletier, eighty-six, who lives alone in a cabin at Allagash. Dennis never heard of cabin fever. How does he pass the time? He grins. "I just go out snowshoeing every day."

That's how it is with Maine people. Let a winter be cruel and a livelihood uncertain and disaster imminent. They see things through. They hang in there somehow, year in, year out, caught up in this incredibly masochistic love affair with adversity. They "make do," or come up with "something just as good as something better." And somehow there's always time to keep the Sunday window bright with potted geraniums.

When you get right down to it, Maine people love their land too much to leave it. Those who leave it, they'll tell you, those who give up and head for less wearisome climates of spirit and sustenance and weather, simply do not love it enough.

LIST OF PLATES